SHEPHERD'S NOTES

Shepherd's Notes Titles Available

SHEPHERD'S NOTES COMMENTARY SERIES

Old Testament

0-80549-028-0	Genesis	0-80549-341-7	Psalms 101-150
0-80549-056-6	Exodus	0-80549-016-7	Proverbs
0-80549-069-8	Leviticus & Numbers	0-80549-059-0	Ecclesiastes, Song of
0-80549-027-2	Deuteronomy		Solomon
0-80549-058-2	Joshua & Judges	0-80549-197-X	Isaiah
0-80549-057-4	Ruth & Esther	0-80549-070-1	Jeremiah-
0-80549-063-9	1 & 2 Samuel		Lamentations
0-80549-007-8	1 & 2 Kings	0-80549-078-7	Ezekiel
0-80549-064-7	1 & 2 Chronicles	0-80549-015-9	Daniel
0-80549-194-5	Ezra, Nehemiah	0-80549-326-3	Hosea-Obadiah
0-80549-006-X	Job	0-80549-334-4	Jonah-Zephaniah
0-80549-339-5	Psalms 1-50	0-80549-065-5	Haggai-Malachi
0-80549-340-9	Psalms 51-100		

New Testament

1-55819-688-9	Matthew	1-55819-689-7	Philippians,
0-80549-071-X	Mark		Colossians, &
0-80549-004-3	Luke		Philemon
1-55819-693-5	John	0-80549-000-0	1 & 2 Thessalonians
1-55819-691-8	Acts	1-55819-692-7	1 & 2 Timothy, Titus
0-80549-005-1	Romans	0-80549-336-0	Hebrews
0-80549-325-5	1 Corinthians	0-80549-018-3	James
0-80549-335-2	2 Corinthians	0-80549-019-1	1 & 2 Peter & Jude
1-55819-690-0	Galatians	0-80549-214-3	1, 2 & 3 John
0-80549-327-1	Ephesians	0-80549-017-5	Revelation

SHEPHERD'S NOTES CHRISTIAN CLASSICS

0-80549-347-6	Mere Christianity-C.S.Lewis	0-80549-394-8	Miracles-C.S.Lewis
0-80549-353-0	The Problem of Pain/ A Grief Observed-C.S.Lewis	0-80549-196-1	Lectures to My Students-Charles Haddon Spurgeon
0-80549-199-6	The Confessions-Augustine	0-80549-220-8	The Writings of Justin Martyr
0-80549-200-3	Calvin's Institutes	0-80549-345-X	The City of God

SHEPHERD'S NOTES-BIBLE SUMMARY SERIES

0-80549-377-8	Old Testament	0-80549-385-9	Life & Letters of Paul
0-80549-378-6	New Testament	0-80549-376-X	Manners & Customs
0-80549-384-0	Life & Teachings of Jesus		of Bible Times
		0-80549-380-8	Basic Christian Beliefs

SHEPHERD'S NOTES

When you need a guide through the Scriptures

Ephesians

HOLMAN
REFERENCE

Nashville, Tennessee

Shepherd Notes—*Ephesians*

© 1998 Broadman & Holman Publishers, Nashville, Tennessee

All rights reserved

Printed in the United States of America

ISBN 0–8054–9327–1

Dewey Decimal Classification: 227.5

Subject Heading: BIBLE. N.T. EPHESIANS

Library of Congress Card Catalog Number: 98–15305

Library of Congress Cataloging-in Publication Data

Ephesians / Dana Gould, editor.

      p. cm. — (Shepherd's notes)

    Includes bibliographical references.

    ISBN 0–8054–9327–1

    1. Bible. N.T. Ephesians—Study and teaching.

I. Gould Dana. 1951– . II. Series.

BS2695.5.E64 1998   98–15305

227'.507—dc21   CIP

5 6 7 8   08 07 06 05

CONTENTS

Dear Reader:

Shepherd's Notes are designed to give you a quick, step-by-step over-view of every book of the Bible. They are not meant to be substitutes for the biblical text; rather, they are study guides intended to help you explore the wisdom of Scripture in personal or group study and to apply that wisdom successfully in your own life.

Shepherd's Notes guide you through the main themes of each book of the Bible and illuminate fascinating details through appropriate commentary and reference notes. Historical and cultural background information brings the Bible into sharper focus.

Six different icons, used throughout the series, call your attention to historical-cultural information, Old Testament and New Testament references, word pictures, unit summaries, and personal application for everyday life.

Whether you are a novice or a veteran at Bible study, I believe you will find *Shepherd's Notes* a resource that will take you to a new level in your mining and applying the riches of Scripture.

In Him,

David R. Shepherd
Editor-in-Chief

DESIGNED FOR THE BUSY USER

Shepherd's Notes for Ephesians is designed to provide an easy-to-use tool for getting a quick handle on this Bible book's important features, and for gaining an understanding of the message of Ephesians. Information available in more difficult-to-use reference works has been incorporated into the *Shepherd's Notes* format. This brings you the benefits of many more advanced and expensive works packed into one small volume.

Shepherd's Notes are for laymen, pastors, teachers, small-group leaders and participants, as well as the classroom student. Enrich your personal study or quiet time. Shorten your class or small-group preparation time as you gain valuable insights into the truths of God's Word that you can pass along to your students or group members.

DESIGNED FOR QUICK ACCESS

Those with time constraints will especially appreciate the time-saving features built in the *Shepherd's Notes*. All features are intended to aid a quick and concise encounter with the heart of the message of this important book.

Concise Commentary. Ephesians provides a vision of what God is doing in the world and invites believers to join Him in that work.

Outlined Text. A comprehensive outline covers the entire text of Ephesians. This is a valuable feature for following the narrative's flow, allowing for a quick, easy way to locate a particular passage.

Shepherd's Notes. These summary statements appear at the close of every key section of the narrative. While functioning in part as a quick summary, they also deliver the essence of the message presented in the sections they cover.

Icons. Various icons in the margin highlight recurring themes in Ephesians, aiding in selective searching or tracing of those themes.

Sidebars and Charts. These specially selected features provide additional background information to your study or preparation. These include definitions as well as cultural, historical, and biblical insights.

Maps. These are placed at appropriate places in the book to aid your understanding and study of a text or passage.

Questions to Guide Your Study. These thought-provoking questions and discussion starters are designed to encourage interaction with the truth and principles of God's Word.

In addition to the above features, study aids have been included at the back of the book for those readers who require or desire more information and resources for working through Ephesians. These include: chapter outlines for studying Ephesians and a list of reference sources used for this volume, which offer many works that allow the reader to extend the scope of his or her study of Ephesians.

DESIGNED TO WORK FOR YOU

Personal Study. Using the Shepherd's Notes with a passage of Scripture can enlighten your study and take it to a new level. At your fingertips is information that would require searching several volumes to find. In addition, many points of application occur throughout the volume, contributing to personal growth.

Teaching. Outlines frame the text of Ephesians and provide a logical presentation of the message. *Shepherd's Notes* provide summary statements for presenting the essence of key points and events. Personal Application icons point out personal application of the message of Ephesians, and Historical Context icons indicate where background information is supplied.

Group Study. Shepherd's Notes can be an excellent companion volume to use for gaining a quick but accurate understanding of the book of Ephesians. Each group member can benefit by having his or her own copy. The *Note's* format accommodates the study of or the tracing of the themes throughout Ephesians. Leaders may use this book's flexible features to prepare for group sessions, or during group sessions. Questions to Guide Your Study can spark discussion of the key points and truths of Ephesians.

LIST OF MARGIN ICONS USED IN EPHESIANS

Shepherd's Notes. Placed at the end of each section, a capsule statement provides the reader with the essence of the message of that section.

Old Testament Reference. To indicate a prophecy fulfillment and its discussion in the text.

New Testament Reference. Used when the writer refers to New Testament passages that are related to or have a bearing on the passage's understanding or interpretation.

Historical Background. Historical Context. To indicate historical information—historical, biographical, cultural— and provide insight on the understanding or interpretation of a passage.

Personal Application. Used when the text provides a personal or universal application of truth.

Word Picture. Indicates that the meaning of a specific word or phrase is illustrated so as to shed light on it.

Ephesians is a special New Testament book. Here the teachings of Paul find their highest expression in a sweeping summary of his faith. This letter to the Christians at Ephesus is the one that best sets out the basic concepts of the Christian faith. An insightful and powerful book, Ephesians is both devotional and theological, holding a place all its own among Paul's New Testament letters.

EPHESIANS IN A NUTSHELL

Purpose:	To emphasize the unity of the church in Christ through the power of the Spirit
Major Doctrine:	Re-creation of the human family as God originally intended it
Key Passage:	Eph. 1:10: "To bring all things in heaven and on earth together under one head"
Other Key Doctrines:	Predestination, reconciliation, and union with Christ

AUTHOR

Paul the apostle referred to himself as the author in two places in the letter: 1:1 and 3:1. Some scholars think Ephesians contains a writing style, vocabulary, and even some teachings that are not typical of the apostle Paul. Yet others regard the book of Ephesians as the crown of all of Paul's writings. In line with the undisputed acceptance of Pauline authorship in the early church, we can conclude that there is no reason to dispute Paul as author of Ephesians.

Paul was the outstanding missionary and writer of the early church. Both he and his theology are important in the New Testament, not only because thirteen epistles bear his name, but also because of the extended biographical information given in the book of Acts. From the information in these two sources, we can piece together a picture of one of the major personalities of early Christianity. The letters of Paul, as listed in the New Testament, include Romans through Philemon. His experience of radical change and call to proclaim the gospel to the Gentiles provided his motivation to travel throughout the Roman world, preaching the way of Christ.

PURPOSE FOR WRITING

Paul wrote most of his letters to meet specific needs in the churches, but it is difficult to determine the specific occasion for which Ephesians was written.

The letter itself, however, hints at several purposes. The apostle taught that Jewish and Gentile believers are one in Christ. This oneness is to be demonstrated by their love for one another. Paul used the noun form of the verb "to love" (*agapē*) nineteen times (about one-sixth of the total uses in all of Paul's letters). Ephesians begins with love (1:4–6) and ends with love (6:23–24).

Ephesians is a general statement of Christian truth concerning the church, Christian unity, and the Christian walk. The understanding of this truth is as necessary for the church today as it was in Paul's day.

DATE AND PLACE OF WRITING

Interpreters are divided on the question of the time and place of the writing of Ephesians. Paul's imprisonments in Acts 21:15–26:32 and 27:1–28:31 are the only ones that might bear on the question of where and when the Prison Epistles (Ephesians, Colossians, Philemon, Philippians) were written. In all four of these letters, Paul mentioned his imprisonment.

Date. The traditional view is that Ephesians was written during the early sixties (60–62). References in Ephesians 6:21–22 suggest that Tychicus carried the letter to its destination.

Place. Careful review of this extensive and complex issue leaves the subjective opinion that all four Prison Epistles were written from Rome while Paul was imprisoned there about A.D. 60–62.

AUDIENCE

In spite of the traditional heading (1:1), relatively little is known about the recipients of the letter who are called "Ephesians." (Several important and early manuscripts do not contain the words "in Ephesus" (v. 1).

Some interpreters have suggested the Ephesians was originally a circular letter, sent perhaps to churches throughout Asia. The church at Ephesus kept a copy of this letter without an address. As time passed, readers outside Ephesus might have assumed that Ephesus had received the letter initially. The hypothesis of a circular letter, though not without problems, provides the most logical explanation of the omission of "in Ephesus" from the greetings of the letter.

Tychicus

Tychicus, whose name means "fortunate," was one of Paul's fellow workers in the ministry. Tychicus and Onesiumus carried the Colossian letter from Paul, they were also the bearers of this letter to Ephesus. Tradition holds that Tychicus died a martyr.

PAUL'S MINISTRY AT EPHESUS

At the close of his second missionary journey (about A.D. 49–52), Paul left Achaia (Greece), taking Aquila and Priscilla with him. They stopped at Ephesus and surveyed the situation in that city where religions flourished. The Ephesians urged Paul to stay, but he declined. Leaving Aquila and Priscilla and perhaps Timothy there to carry on the Christian witness (Acts 18:18–21), Paul sailed to Antioch. He returned to Ephesus during a third missionary journey and experienced triumph over the challenge of Jewish religious leaders as well as that of the Greco-Roman religions represented in the worship of the Greek goddess Artemis (Roman name, Diana; Acts 19:24).

Paul's ministry in Ephesus lasted three years (Acts 20:31). From there he journeyed to Jerusalem, where he was arrested by the Jews and turned over to the Romans.

STRUCTURE OF THE LETTER

Ephesians follows the pattern common to Paul's letters—discussing doctrine in the first half, followed by practice in the second half. The content of Ephesians falls naturally into two divisions:

1. Chapters 1–3 discuss the spiritual privileges of the church, spelling out the great Christian truths of experience and belief.
2. Chapters 4–6 present the responsibilities of believers in their Christian walk in light of the truths of the first three chapters.

Unique Features of Ephesians. Although Ephesians and Colossians contain many similarities, it is important to observe the distinctives of Ephesians. When the content of Ephesians that is common to Colossians is removed, units of material that are unique to Ephesians remains, as the following chart shows.

Similar Passages in Ephesians and Colossians

	EPHESIANS	COLOSSIANS
Christ as head of the church	1:23	1:18
Domestic responsibilities of believers	5:22–6:9	3:18–4:1

Distinctives in Ephesians

PASSAGE	TOPIC
1:3–14	An expanded benediction
2:1–10	A confessional statement on the new life
3:14–21	A prayer to understand the mystery of Christ
4:1–16	An extended exhortation to Christian unity
5:8–14	A section on walking in the light
5:23–32	A theological expansion on the household roles
6:10–17	A unique picture of the Christian's spiritual warfare

LITERARY FEATURES IN EPHESIANS

A Comparison of Ephesians and Colossians. The salutation and structure of Ephesians is similar to Colossians. Many of the same topics are treated in both letters, and the message is strikingly similar. Of the 155 verses in Ephesians, more than half contain expressions identical with those in Colossians. While Colossians is abrupt, argumentative, and seemingly compressed, Ephesians presents a bigger, finished picture that is meditative, instructive, and expansive.

THE THEOLOGY OF EPHESIANS

Doctrinal Emphasis

INTRO

Central to the message of Ephesians is the re-creation of the human family according to God's original intention. The new creation destroys the misguided view of some people that God accepts the Jew and rejects the Gentile. Paul claimed that this distinction was abolished at Christ's sacrificial death. Thus, a hindrance no longer remains to reuniting all humanity as the people of God, with Christ as the head (1:22–23). The new body—the church—has been endowed by the power of the Holy Spirit to enable them to live out their new life (1:3–2:10) and put into practice the new standards (4:1–6:9).

Theological Significance of Paul's Letter to the Ephesians

This letter lifts its readers to a new vantage point from which they are united with the risen and ascended Christ. Believers are not to have a limited or merely earthly perspective. When we view life from the heavenly realms (1:3), we can understand that the church's strength is not in human resources but in the grace and strength of God.

The church, God's people, does not function just to carry out routine activities. It reveals the wisdom of God and proclaims the rich redemption provided by Jesus Christ (1:3–11; 3:2–13). This grand letter gives us a purpose for living in line with God's history (1:10). This is accomplished as we live in submission to Christ, the head of the church, and indeed the supreme authority over all things (1:22).

THE RELEVANCE OF EPHESIANS FOR BELIEVERS TODAY

Ephesians has been called the most modern of all the New Testament writings. The breadth and depth of its doctrinal teachings make it a lively source of ideas for every situation. Its emphasis on the inclusive nature of the church makes it a rich source of inspiration and challenge for churches of any age.

Christ for the Whole Universe

Ephesians is one of the major sources for our vision of Christ as the Lord of all creation. Although New Testament writers could not have envisioned our modern technology, they had no doubt that Christ was big enough to be Lord of the entire creation. He was "far above all rule and authority, power and dominion, and every title that can be given, not only in the present age but also in the one to come. And God placed all things under his feet and appointed him to be head over everything for the church, which is his body, the fullness of him who fills everything in every way" (Eph. 1:21–22).

Ephesians rekindles our vision of the church as the body of Christ in which gifts are recognized and leaders equip people for the work of the ministry.

The Nature and Purpose of the Church

No biblical book provides a higher view of the church than Ephesians, and none has had a greater impact on modern church life and theory.

Bringing Together a Divided World

From Ephesians we learn that God's plan is "to bring all things in heaven and on earth together under one head" (Eph. 1:10). Paul's letter sets forth a church in which both Jews and Gentiles join in one faith, serving one Lord. Paul's message of peace and unified purpose in Christ is both relevant and pertinent to the modern world.

A Sense of Calling

Ephesians challenges its readers to their best with Paul's exhortation to "live a life worthy of the calling you have received" (4:1). Institutions, organizations, and individuals often lack a sense of purpose. Even churches sometimes languish because they lack a compelling goal. The view of life offered by Ephesians is a powerful motivation for believers to get involved in what God is doing in the world.

Worthy Living

In today's pluralistic culture where moral values are widely questioned and abandoned, Ephesians describes Christian living as walking in the light in the midst of a world of darkness. It presents a radically different lifestyle for Christians and describes appropriate patterns of behavior in detail.

The Life and Ministry of Paul

MAJOR EVENTS	BIBLICAL RECORDS		POSSIBLE DATES
	ACTS	GALATIANS	
Birth			A.D. 1
Conversion	9:1–25	1:11–17	A.D. 33
First Jerusalem visit	9:26–30	1:18–20	A.D. 36
Famine	11:25–30	2:1–10?	A.D. 46
First missionary journey	13:1 to 14:28		A.D. 47–48
Apostolic council in Jerusalem	15:1–29	2:1–10?	A.D. 49
Second missionary journey	15:36 to 18:21		
Letter to the Galatians			A.D. 53–55
Third missionary journey	18:23 to 21:6		A.D. 53–57
Letters to the Corinthians			A.D. 55
Arrest and prison in Jerusalem and Caesarea	21:8 to 26:32		A.D. 57
Prison in Rome	27:1 to 28:30		A.D. 60–62
Letter to the Ephesians			A.D. 60–62
Death			A.D. 67

QUESTIONS TO GUIDE YOUR STUDY

1. What prompted Paul to write his letter to the Ephesians?
2. What was Paul's goal for this letter?
3. What is the major doctrine of this letter? What are some of its other themes?
4. What is the relevance of Ephesians to the believer today?

BASIC OUTLINE FOR EPHESIANS

I. Introduction (1:1–2)
II. God's Purposes in Christ (1:3–3:21)
III. God's Purposes in the Church (4:1–6:20)
IV. Conclusion (6:21–24)

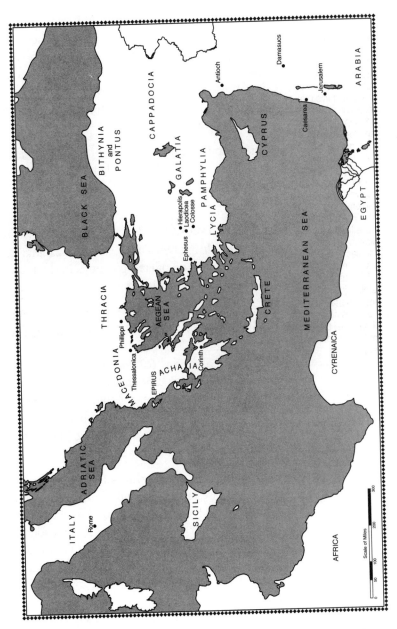

Taken from Richard R. Melick, *Philippians, Colossians, Philemon*, vol. 32, New American Commentary (Nashville, Tenn.: Broadman & Holman Publishers, 1992), p. 37.

EPHESIANS 1

Generally, Paul's Epistles follow the normal pattern of the Hellenistic letter, the basic form of which consists of five major sections:
1. Opening (sender, addressee, greeting)
2. Thanksgiving or blessing (often with prayer of intercession, well wishes, or personal greetings)
3. The burden of the letter (including citation of classical sources and arguments)
4. Parenesis (ethical instruction, and exhortation)
5. Closing (mention of personal plans, mutual friends, and benediction)

In this first chapter, Paul focused on the spiritual blessings Christians have because they are in Christ. The chapter breaks down into two major sections: (1) the blessings of the believer in Christ, and (2) Paul's prayer that believers might understand these blessings and the power they can bring to one's life.

The opening words of the letter to the Ephesians are in the standard form for letters in New Testament times. This form is known as the *Hellenistic letter*.

SALUTATION (1:1–2)

Paul introduced himself by name and calling. In his salutation, he offered greetings in the manner common to all his letters.

Name. The author declared himself to be Paul, which scholars take as a reference to the apostle Paul. Tradition supports Paul as author, and many scholars see 6:20 as internal evidence pointing to Paul. A unique feature of this salutation is the absence of any mention of Paul's companions. Usually, Paul included the names of those who were accompanying him at the time of writing.

Calling. Paul refered to himself as an "apostle." This term describes "one who is sent." It is what we would call a missionary. His reference to his apostleship served two purposes: (1) it identified him as one on a mission from Christ, and (2) it pointed to his authority to speak as a leader. Because he was an apostle "by the will of God," his apostleship came not through any human agent. The will of God is a major theme that Paul expands upon in his letter.

Paul's Readers. Paul addressed his letter to the "saints" in Ephesus. *Saints* are those who are "set apart for God," which designates them as God's people. As for the demographics of the church at Ephesus, we know relatively little.

City of Ephesus

One of the largest and most impressive cities in the ancient world, Ephesus was a political, religious, and commercial center in Asia Minor. In association with the ministries of Paul, Timothy and the apostle John played a significant role in the spread of early Christianity. Ephesus and its inhabitants are mentioned more than twenty times in the New Testament.

The ancient city of Ephesus was located in western Asia Minor at the mouth of the Cayster River and was an important seaport. Ephesus was situated between the Maeander River to the south and the Hermus River to the north; it had excellent access to both river valleys, which allowed it to flourish as a commercial center. Due to the accumulation of silt deposited by the river, the present site of the city is approximately five to six miles inland.

The earliest inhabitants of Ephesus were groups called Leleges and Carians, who were driven out around 1000 B.C. by Ionian Greek settlers lead by Androclus of Athens. The new inhabitants of Ephesus assimilated the native religion of the area, the worship of a goddess of fertility whom they identified with the Greek goddess Artemis—the virgin huntress. (Later, the Romans identified Artemis with their goddess Diana.)

Alexander the Great, who was reportedly born on the same day as the Artemision fire, took over the area in 334 B.C. His offer to finance the ongoing reconstruction of the temple was diplomatically declined. The rebuilt temple, completed about 250 B.C., became known as one of the seven wonders of the ancient world. One of Alexander's generals, Lysimachus, ruled Ephesus from about 301 B.C. to 281 B.C., when he was killed by Seleucus I. Ephesus remained under control of the Seleucids until their defeat by the Romans in 189 B.C. Rome gave the city to the king of Pergamum as a reward for his military assistance. In 133 B.C., at the death of the last Pergamum ruler, the city came under direct Roman control.

Under the Romans, Ephesus thrived, reaching the pinnacle of its greatness during the first and second centuries of the Christian era. At the time of Paul, Ephesus was probably the fourth largest city in the world, with a population of about 250,000. During the reign of the emperor Hadrian, Ephesus was designated the capital of the Roman province of Asia. The grandeur of the ancient city is evident in the remains uncovered by archaeologists, including the ruins of the Artemision, the civic agora, the temple of Domitian, gymnasiums, public baths, a theater with seating for 24,000 people, a library, and the commercial agora, as well as several streets and private residences. Also discovered were the head and forearm of a huge statue of the emperor Domitian. Today, the Turkish town of Seljuk occupies the site of ancient Ephesus.

■ *Paul identified himself by name and calling.*
■ *He offered greetings in the manner common*
■ *to his letters. Absent is the usual mention of*
■ *Paul's companions. Also absent in the earlier*
■ *manuscript copies of Ephesians is the*
■ *address "in Ephesus."*

BLESSINGS IN CHRIST (1:3–14)

God the Father's Purpose (vv. 3–6)

Paul began his letter with a great statement of praise to God for His blessings in Christ. This section is one long sentence in the original text, made up of carefully balanced clauses. This extended benediction surveys the redemptive activity of the triune God. The grand theme of this section is God's eternal purpose in history (v. 9). (Some have seen here a hymn of three stanzas: vv. 3–6, vv. 7–12, and vv. 13–14, with each stanza concluding with a reference to the praise of God's glorious grace.)

> We are blessed with spiritual blessings "in Christ" (v. 3).

The expression "in Christ" occurs some thirty-five times in Ephesians. The motive behind God's plan is love. His loving purpose aims at personal relationship.

God has chosen us (vv. 3–4).

To "choose" means to "call out, select." God has claimed those in Christ for Himself and His own purpose. Commenting on this passage, A. T. Robertson says that it is a "definitive statement of God's elective grace concerning believers in Christ" (*Word Pictures in the New Testament,* "Epistles of Paul," vol. 4, 517). Although this is

"*Blessed* be the God ... who has *blessed* us ... with every spiritual *blessing*" (v. 3).

The word translated "bless" is a compound of two words: "well" and "a word." Its literal, root meaning is "to speak well of." The NIV translates the opening phrase of verse 3 as, "praise be to the God." But the NRSV translation, "blessed be the God," maintains Paul's original word play. Paul uses a form of this word three times in verse 3, as noted by A. T. Robertson. "Paul lovingly plays with the idea. The believer is a citizen of heaven and the spiritual blessings count the most for him" (*Word Pictures in the New Testament,* "Epistles of Paul," vol. 4, 517). When we address this word toward God, it is an acknowledgment of His attribute of goodness.

Chose

The word Paul uses here—"chose"—is a compound word in the original text. It is made up of the preposition "out of" prefixed to the verb "to call, say, or tell." It is translated "to pick out, select." Given the grammatical elements of the word in this context, it means that God *Himself* chose us.

Adoption

Regarding the New Testament concept of adoption, William Barclay said, "The person who had been adopted had all the rights of a legitimate son in his new family and completely lost all rights in his old family. In the eyes of the law, he was a new person. So new was he that even all debts and obligations connected with his previous family were abolished as if they had never existed. That is what Paul says that God has done for us" (The Letter to the Galatians and Ephesians [Philadelphia: Westminster, 1976], 80).

difficult to comprehend, God has chosen us to be His own.

God has adopted us (v. 5).
Here the use of *adoption* is a family concept. It involves the placing of a family member into the privileges and blessings of adulthood.

God has graciously favored us (v. 6).
Although unacceptable to God by our own merits, God has accepted us through Christ. Paul declared, "To the praise of his glorious grace, which he has freely given us in the One he loves." God has generously favored us by giving many provisions of His grace.

■ *Paul began by discussing the blessings of*
■ *Christ as they relate to God the Father's pur-*
■ *poses. He chose us before the creation of the*
■ *world to be adopted and accepted through his*
■ *Son Jesus Christ.*

God the Son's Accomplishments (vv. 7–10)
In this section we see three of the greatest concepts of the Christian faith:

- deliverance from the penalty of sin;
- forgiveness of sins; and
- understanding of the will of God.

Christ has redeemed us (v. 7a).
Redemption is a term that occurs throughout the Old Testament. The idea of redemption is vitally related to the themes of liberation, deliverance, and ransom. Within this model we see a struggle between the kingdom of God and the hostile powers enslaving humankind. Redemption is the idea of bringing sinners out of hostile bondage into authentic freedom (Col. 2:15). As

Redeemer, Jesus breaks the power of sin and creates a new and obedient heart by delivering us from the powers of sin, guilt, death, and Satan. He brings about a people who have been bought with a price (1 Pet. 1:18–19).

Christ has forgiven us (7b).

The word for *forgiveness* means "to send forth, send away." It refers to the removal of a person's sins. This word for "trespasses" is the term for false steps or a deviation from the right.

Christ has revealed God's will to us (vv. 8–10).

This passage reaches its high point as Paul reveals what God has made known in Christ. It is the "mystery of his will." *Mystery* was a word common to Paul's readers. In the first century, cults known as mystery religions were built around secret spiritual lore known only to a few people. Some of these religions advanced the idea that salvation was offered to a select few who shared in their special knowledge. Paul countered this teaching in this letter and in his letter to the Colossians.

The mystery Paul spoke of is not something hidden, but something "made known." It was a mystery in the sense that it was previously unknown. It could only be known by a revelation from God. In Christ, such a revelation is available. The content of the mystery was the will and purpose of God. This purpose was set forth in Christ. Apart from Christ, the contents of the mystery could not be known. Only as people receive Christ and begin to see life in the light of His revelation do they realize what God is working to accomplish in human lives.

In describing the believer's understanding of the mystery of God's will, Paul used two terms that are synonyms. Although similar in meaning, these terms were distinguished by Paul's Greek readers:

1. *Wisdom* is the ability to see into the heart of things and understand them. It is the knowledge that satisfies the intellect.
2. *Understanding* is insight that leads to wise action. It enables a person to handle the day-to-day problems of practical life and living.

The right time

The word Paul used for "time" (*kairos*) speaks of a particular time of opportunity, not simply the passing of days and years.

Paul explained that God's making known the mystery of His will is part of His pursuing a plan for "when the times will have reached their fulfillment" (v . 10). God will accomplish His strategy when the time is right.

God plans to unite all things in Christ. When the time is right, God will "bring all things in heaven and on earth together under one head, even Christ" (v. 10). Paul declared that all of reality—physical and spiritual—will be included in the unity of Christ.

Christ has made us an inheritance (vv. 11–12).

To bring all things . . . together

The phrase "to bring together" is only one word in the original text, but it is loaded with meaning. It refers to the process of gathering something together to present as a whole. In the New Testament, it is used only here and in Rom. 13:9, where Paul summed up the Commandments into one rule: "Love your neighbor as yourself."

Verse 11 in the *New Revised Standard Version* reads, "In Christ we have also obtained an inheritance." The word Paul used here literally means, "we were *made* an inheritance" (italics added). Not only has God given us an inheritance in Christ (1 Pet. 1:3–4); He has also given us as an inheritance for Christ! The church is His body and bride and will share in His glory.

■ *The believer's blessings in Christ include the*
■ *Son's redemptive work. The believer has*
■ *been redeemed and forgiven by Christ.*
■ *Through Him, God's will is revealed. As His*
■ *body, temple, and bride, Christ also has*
■ *made us an inheritance that He will someday*
■ *claim for Himself.*

God the Spirit's Ministry (vv. 13–14)

The sealing of the Spirit occurs at the time of believing: "When you heard the word of truth" (v. 13). Those "also included" (v. 13) were the Gentiles. Paul's change of pronouns from "we" to "you" indicates that he was referring to second-generation converts of the Christian message—Gentiles.

The Spirit has given us a deposit (v. 14).

Deposit is a business term used for money given as a down payment for a purchase. Because we as believers have not entered into our final salvation, God has given us the Holy Spirit as a deposit, a down payment, to assure us that the "goods" will be delivered. Through the Spirit we have an advance experience of what we will have fully in heaven.

■ *The blessings in Christ involve the ministry*
■ *of God the Spirit. The Spirit has sealed us,*
■ *ensuring God's ownership of us. The Spirit is*
■ *also our earnest, our down payment on the*
■ *fulfillment of salvation that is yet to come.*

Deposit

This is a word of Semitic origin (possibly Phoenician). It has a common use in the papyri as earnest money in a purchase for a cow or for a wife (a dowry). In the New Testament, the word appears only in 2 Cor. 1:22 and Eph. 1:14. "It is a part payment on the total obligation, and we use the very expression today, 'earnest money.' It is God, says Paul, who has done all this for us and the Spirit is God's pledge that He is sincere. This earnest deposit of the Spirit in our hearts is the witness of the Spirit that we are God's" (Taken from A. T. Robertson, *Word Pictures in the New Testament*, "Epistles of Paul," Vol. 4, 214).

The Believer's Blessings in Christ

BLESSING	EXPLANATION
Chosen (v. 4)	God claims those in Christ for Himself and His own purpose
Adopted (v. 5)	The placing of a family member into the privileges and blessings of adulthood
Graciously favored (v. 6)	The grace of God freely given to those in Christ
Redeemed (v. 7)	The purchase of our deliverance was made at a great cost: "through his blood"
Forgiven (v. 7)	The removal of one's sins
Revealed God's will to us (v. 9)	What God has made known in Christ
Made us an inheritance (v. 11)	God has given those in Christ as an inheritance for Christ, and they will share in His glory.
Sealed (v. 13)	God owns those in Christ and will keep them
Gave the Holy Spirit as a deposit (v. 14)	God has given the Holy Spirit as a guarantee of the future glory to come

The Spirit has sealed us (v. 13).

A seal was a mark, perhaps on wax, which showed that a letter or a delivery was authentic and had been delivered intact. "Seals were used as a guarantee indicating not only ownership but also to guarantee the correctness of the contents (see 2 Cor. 1:22)" (Fritz Rienecker, *Linguistic Key to the Greek New Testament* [Grand Rapids: Zondervan, 1980], 523). Sealing means that God owns us and will keep us.

PAUL'S PRAYER FOR HIS READERS (1:15–23)

Paul's entire letter to the Ephesians was written within the framework of prayer. This section functions as an extended prayer.

Paul's Reason for Praying (vv. 15–16)

Although Paul may not have known his readers personally, he had heard of their faith and love, perhaps through Epaphras, as in Colossians 1:4–8. Whatever Paul's relationship with these Christians, he prayed for them in this passage. His prayers were continuous and intense, characterized by thanksgiving.

Paul's Prayer Requests

REQUEST	STATEMENT
1. That his readers might know that God had called them to a great hope (v. 18)	"*What is* the hope to which he has called you" (NRSV)
2. That his readers might know the quality and extent of their blessings in Christ (v. 18)	"*What are* the riches of his glorious inheritance" (NRSV)
3. That his readers might understand and experience the power of God (v. 19)	"*What is* the immeasurable greatness of his power" (NRSV)

Paul's Prayer for His Readers' Understanding (vv. 17–19)

Paul's prayer was addressed to God in His relation to Jesus Christ as in 1:3. He further described Him as "the Father of glory," probably meaning "the all-glorious Father" (NEB). This is in line with Paul's emphasis in this chapter on the fullness and richness of God's nature and blessings.

In his prayer, we see three objects of the knowledge Paul desired for his readers. Paul introduced the content of each request with the words "what is" or "what are." (Although the *New International Version* does not translate these words, other versions such as the *New Revised Standard Version* do.) As A. T. Robertson commented, "Note three indirect questions after "to know" (what is the hope, what the riches, and what the surpassing greatness). When the Holy Spirit opens the eyes of the heart, one will be able to see all these great truths" (*Word Pictures in the New Testament*, "Epistles of Paul," vol. 4, 521).

Paul made three requests for the Ephesian believers:

1. *He wanted them to know that God had called them to a great hope (v. 18).* Paul emphasized the origin of their calling and urged them to take part in it.

2. *He wanted them to realize the quality and the extent of the blessings they had in Christ (v. 18).* Paul has already described these blessings as an inheritance (v. 14). That they are an inheritance emphasizes the fact that they are received as a gift and already guaranteed, even though they are not yet fully bestowed upon believers.

3. *He wanted them to understand and experience the power of God (v. 19).* God's power is unlimited—a concept we cannot fully understand. What Paul wanted to convey to his readers is that God is at work in the life of a Christian in a powerful way. By piling up four synonyms for strength, Paul strained the limits of language to suggest something that cannot be put into words.

Being aware of our calling, our blessing, and our empowerment will impact the way we live everyday.

Synonyms for Power in Ephesians 1:19

ENGLISH TERM	GREEK WORD	EXPANDED MEANING
Power	*dunameos*	Inherent ability; ability to perform anything
Working	*energeian*	The effectual working of ability
Mighty	*kratous*	Strength in relation to an end to be gained or dominion to be exercised
Strength	*ischuos*	Strength that a person has; power in possession, ability, or latent power

What God Has Done for Us in Christ (vv. 20–23)

The mention of God's great power in verse 19 led Paul to expound upon the greatest demonstration of that power—the *resurrection*. When Old Testament writers spoke of God's power, they referred to the Exodus from Egypt and the creation of the world. New Testament writers, however, pointed to the resurrection. Paul referred to this in Phil. 3:10 as "the power of his resurrection."

As a result of His resurrection, Jesus is now enthroned at the right hand of God, a position

Think about the tremendous power and creativity that transformed Jesus' lifeless body into a body that transcends space as we know it and can never be again subject to death. What difference does it make to realize that this same power is with you?

of greatest honor and authority. God has put all powers in existence at His feet. Christ is now the head of all things.

In verse 22, we have the first use of the word *church* in Ephesians. Paul declared that Christ is the head of the church. Not only is Christ the church's guide and authority, but Paul explained that Christ and His church exist in an organic unity. Paul closed this chapter by describing the church as "his body, the fullness of him who fills everything in every way." Although interpreted variously, this statement seems to mean that Christ fills everything and that God wants the church to be the full expression of Christ.

■ *Paul prayed for his readers and made three*
■ *requests on their behalf: (1) he wanted them*
■ *to know that God had called them to a great*
■ *hope; (2) he wanted them to realize the*
■ *quality and the extent of the blessings they*
■ *had in Christ; and (3) he wanted them to*
■ *have an understanding and experience of the*
■ *power of God.*

QUESTIONS TO GUIDE YOUR STUDY

1. In what sense does God choose Christians? What does this tell us about God's true character?

2. The grand theme of verses 3–14 is God's eternal purpose in history (v. 9). How does each of God's spiritual blessings help accomplish that purpose?

3. Paul prayed for his readers. What is the content of his requests on their behalf?

4. In verse 19, Paul used four synonyms to describe God's strength. What does each contribute to our understanding? What idea or ideas do these collectively convey to the reader?

5. What is the greatest demonstration of God's power? Why is it the greatest?

Paul will return to his theme of the church in 2:11, but in the first section of this chapter he describes the work of Christ in the lives of God's people. Verses 1–10 are one long sentence in the original Greek text, bringing together all of Paul's teachings about grace, faith, and the Christian life.

FROM DEATH TO LIFE (2:1–10)

"Used to live"

The word translated "used to live" (NIV; "once lived," NRSV) is the Greek word for "walk." Here it is a compound word made up of the preposition "around" and the verb "to walk." "Figuratively, it signifies the whole round of activities of the individual life, whether of the unregenerate (Eph. 4:17), or of the believer, 1 Cor. 7:17; Col. 2:6" (*Vine's Complete Expository Dictionary of Old and New Testament Words* [Nashville: Thomas Nelson, 1996], 664). Life is a walk, an active process that moves along step by step.

From Death to Life

THE DEADLY WALK (THE PAST)	THE LIVELY WALK (THE PRESENT)
Dead in trespasses and sins	Alive in Christ
Follows the ways of the world	Walks in the light
Disobedient	Obedient to the Word of God
Gratifies sinful desires	Lives to please God

Dead in Sin (vv. 1–3)

Paul explained that those who are now alive in Christ were not always alive. A look at their former lives would show that they did not have life at all. The tense of the Greek verb for "used to live" summarizes one's total past life as a point. The sum of their past spiritual experience was death.

Paul outlined several characteristics of the past walk of believers:

1. *They were dead in their transgressions and sins (v. 1).*

   "Transgressions" and "sins" are close synonyms but with different backgrounds. *Transgressions* indicates wrong steps taken or a deliberate breaking of the law. To *sin* means "to miss the mark." Paul used these two words together for emphasis by repetition. The sins he speaks of here are not mere isolated acts; they speak of a way of life or a pattern of conduct in which these people had walked.

2. *They followed the ways of this world (v. 2).*

   Powerful factors influenced their deadly walk. First, the "ways of this world" describe the present world order and its present course. The pressures of society and culture led them away from God.

3. *They were disobedient (v. 2).*

   There is a superhuman, spiritual power of evil that generates a spirit of disobedience in people. He is Satan, called here the "ruler of the kingdom of the air" (v. 2). *Air* refers to the spiritual realm. It is important to note that the disobedience Paul mentioned here is our own choice and not simply the effect of Satan on the ways of the world.

4. *They gratified the desires of their sinful nature (v. 3).*

   An important part of our disobedience is rooted in our own sinful desires. These desires originate in our lower, sinful nature. Paul emphasized that this sinful nature involves both the physical body *and* the mind: "desires and thought."

Throughout this passage, Paul emphasized that we all once lived in the way described above: "We were by nature objects of wrath" (v. 3). What he described here is true of every person, Jew or Gentile.

■ *Paul described the human condition and how*
■ *all people were dead in their transgressions*
■ *and sins. They were controlled by their own*
■ *selfish desires and cut off from the life of*
■ *God. As a result, men and women apart from*
■ *Christ were without life, without freedom,*
■ *and without hope.*

The Riches of God's Grace (vv. 4–7)

Against the dark and hopeless background which he described in verses 1–3, Paul changed the entire landscape with the words "but . . . God!" These words signal God's intervention into our hopeless, sinful condition. If it were left up to humankind, there would only be death. But God is not a God of wrath only; He is also a God of mercy. He is "rich in mercy," and His mercy is rooted in His "great love for us."

God shows us His mercy by what He has done in Christ. Believers are brought to life from a state of death. Then they are raised to the presence of God and seated "in the heavenly realms"—or the spiritual realm. In verses 5–7, Paul considered the riches of God's grace.

"Made us alive with Christ" (v. 5).

Christ gives us new life through His resurrection. The word translated "made us alive" is a synonym for "raised," but it also can mean "to keep alive" or "to preserve life." Through Christ, believers are quickened and granted a new spiritual life. (For more on this subject, see Rom. 6:1–10.)

"Raised us up with Christ" (v. 6).
Believers have been raised together with Christ; that is, they have been united with Him in His resurrected life.

"Seated us with him" (v. 6).
Believers sit together with Christ in the heavenly realms. Although believers have yet to be physically resurrected and seated in the heavenlies, spiritually speaking, it has already been accomplished.

■ *By His grace God grants new life to believ-*
■ *ers. The basis for the new life is God's great*
■ *love and mercy. Believers have been reunited*
■ *with Christ in His resurrected life. Formerly,*
■ *people apart from Christ were dead,*
■ *enslaved, and objects of wrath. In Christ,*
■ *believers are now alive, enthroned, and*
■ *objects of God's grace.*

Saved Through Faith (vv. 8–9)
This passage is one of the best summaries of the gospel in the New Testament. It contains many key themes Paul developed elsewhere in his writings, but here he expressed them in a new way to communicate to a wide audience in the Gentile world.

In verses 8–10, Paul focused on three themes:

Grace. The word "grace" occurs twelve times in Ephesians. To the people of Paul's day, it carried the meaning of pleasantness, favor, or gratitude.

"Together with"

Each of the verbs for "made us alive," "raised us," and "seated us" is a compound word. All three have the prepositional prefix "with." God has raised us up with Christ. What happened to Christ will happen to us as we enter into union with Him in Christ. The believer's resurrection, ascension, and enthronement must await complete fulfillment in the resurrection of the body at the end of time, but spiritually this has already happened. Those who are in Christ by faith already share in His fellowship with God.

Early Christians, however, gave this word new significance. They used it to describe the utter generosity that God gives to sinners even though they do not deserve it. This grace is not only forgiveness of sins but the gift of God's power in their lives which brings about a new kind of life.

Salvation. Paul used the term "saved" in these verses to refer to the various aspects of redemption. The grammatical tense he used indicates something accomplished in the past that continues to have results in the present. Paul usually spoke of salvation in more technical terms, such as justification, reconciliation, or adoption. *Saved* is a general term that includes all those various concepts, and it was probably more understandable to Gentiles.

Faith. This is one of Paul's favorite words. It means far more than simply agreeing with an idea. It refers to a total openness to letting God give the benefits of salvation and to obeying the will of God. It is important to note, however, that this does not mean faith is something we do by our own ability. Rather, faith is our willingness to let God into our lives. It includes both trust and commitment.

Paul emphasized that salvation is not something given because of good works. It is not an accomplishment; it is a gift.

The words "and this" (v. 8) are grammatically significant. A. T. Robertson pointed out that the gender of these words is "neuter, not feminine, and so refers not to *faith* (feminine) or to *grace* (feminine also), but to the act of being saved by grace appropriated through faith. Paul shows that salvation does not have its source in men, but in God. Besides, it is God's gift and not the result of our work" (Taken from *Word Pictures in the New Testament*, "Epistles of Paul," vol. 4, 525).

The Believer's Walk

POSITIVELY:	NEGATIVELY:
In newness of life (Rom. 6:4)	Not after the sinful nature (Rom. 8:4)
After the Spirit (Rom. 8:4)	Not after the manner of men (1 Cor. 3:3)
In honesty (Rom. 13:13)	Not in deceptiveness (2 Cor. 4:2)
By faith (2 Cor. 5:7)	Not by sight (2 Cor. 5:7)
In good works (Eph. 2:10)	Not in the vanity of the mind (Eph. 4:17)
In love (Eph. 5:2)	Not disorderly (2 Cor. 12:20)
In wisdom (Col. 4:5)	
In truth (2 John 4)	
After God's commandments (2 John 6)	

For What Purpose (v. 10)

God saves us for a purpose. We are His workmanship. This term "workmanship" can also be translated "handiwork." We are a work of art God is in the process of designing.

This creative process God is carrying out takes place in Christ. We are being made anew for good works.

We are saved from a lot that is negative and destructive, but there is more. We are being

Philippians 2:13 tells us that "it is God who works in you to will and to act according to his good purpose."

saved to do good works. This has been God's plan for us from the beginning, and it's something that begins now. Paul uses one of his phrases here—"that we should walk in them."

Another way of saying this is that God's transforming grace will increasingly result in our doing works that are pleasing to Him as a part of our lives every day.

■ *God spells out His purpose for believers in*
■ *this section. He has restored them. He pro-*
■ *vides salvation as His gift to men and*
■ *women. He then creates a dispensation of*
■ *faith within them so they may receive His*
■ *gracious gift. Salvation is completely God's*
■ *achievement, a pure gift of God.*

UNITY IN CHRIST (2:11–22)

Gentiles Without Hope (vv. 11–12)

The word "therefore" signals a transition is Paul's writing. Paul had been discussing the blessings God gives to the Christian with its emphasis on what Christians as individuals had received in Christ. Beginning here he pointed to Christians as a group. He reminded his Gentile readers that they formerly were not part of the people of God, but in Christ, they had been included.

Paul explained Christ's peace mission in this section. Those who had been separated from the covenant were united, those who had been alienated were reconciled, and those who had been far off were brought near. Paul said they had been "without God" (Greek word *atheos*, v. 12). This is a term from which the word *atheist* is taken. He described them as such even though the pagans had many gods.

Christ Reconciles All (vv. 13–18)

Apart from Christ, the Gentiles were hopeless. "But now in Christ Jesus" (v. 13), Gentiles and Jews are reconciled to God and to one another. The enmity, the barrier, that had existed for hundreds of years has been removed. This is the meaning of reconciliation—*to bring together again.* In Jesus Christ, Jew and Gentile are one because of His work on the cross. Not only has Christ made peace; "he himself is our peace" (v. 14). Jews and Gentiles are no longer strangers; they are called in one hope as one people of God.

A Holy Temple (vv. 19–22)

Only in response to the cross of Christ (called "faith" in 2:8) does peace exists vertically between humans and God and horizontally among humans. Paul called this new society the church.

Paul pictured the church as a nation ("fellow citizens"), a family ("household"), and a "building." This new building is "built on the foundation of the apostles and prophets, with Christ Jesus Himself as the chief cornerstone" (v. 20). The purpose of the church is to become a "dwelling in which God lives by his Spirit" (v. 22).

Reconciliation

Reconciliation involves bringing fallen humanity out of alienation into a state of peace and harmony with God. Jesus, as Reconciler, heals the separation and brokenness created by sin and restores communion between God and humankind. Reconciliation is not a process by which men and women become ever more acceptable to God, Rather, it is an act by which we are delivered from estrangement to fellowship with God. Because of Christ's work on the cross, God has chosen to treat men and women in sin as children rather than transgressors (2 Cor. 5:18–20; Eph. 2:12–16; Col. 1:20–22).

Pictures of the Church in Ephesians 2

PICTURE	REFERENCE	EXPLANATION
As a nation	v. 19a	All believers are God's people—fellow citizens of the "spiritual Israel."
As a family	v. 21b	Both Jews and Gentiles now belong to the household or family of God.
As a building	v. 20–22	God's people are a structure—a temple—where God dwells.

Some modern theologians assert that God has acted in Christ to reconcile all the world to Himself. Consequently, the church's primary concern is not to seek to effect the reconciliation of all people to Christ but merely to proclaim that all have already been reconciled. This kind of universalism is not what Paul teaches in this chapter and is not consistent with his teaching in other letters.

■ *Those who were separated from the covenant*
■ *have been united, those who were alienated*
■ *have been reconciled, and those who were far*
■ *off have been brought near. Jews and Gentiles*
■ *are no longer strangers; they are called in one*
■ *hope as one people of God.*

QUESTIONS TO GUIDE YOUR STUDY

1. Describe the believer's past life of sin and new life in Christ. Why has God saved us from the consequences of our past sins?

2. What riches in Christ does the believer have? Describe them.

3. What was the Gentiles' relationship to God and His promises before Christ?

4. What is the new relationship between the Jews and the Gentiles? How was it established?

5. Paul used three pictures of the church. How does each of these pictures contribute to our understanding of what the church is?

After discussing the union of Jewish and Gentile believers in the church (2:11–22), Paul began to offer a prayer on their behalf. However, he stopped unexpectedly in the middle of his sentence and digressed on the subject of the divine mystery. He did not return to his prayer until verse 14.

THE DIVINE MYSTERY (3:1–13)

Mystery

The ordinary English sense of this word implies knowledge withheld. The biblical sense is *truth revealed*. The word "mystery" refers to what is known by the "initiated." The mystery was made known only by divine revelation and to those illuminated by the Spirit.

The Stewardship of the Mystery (vv. 1–6)

The phrase "for this reason" refers back to the unity of the church in the previous chapter. The point here is that Paul had been given a stewardship. The concept of the Christian as a steward was common in New Testament time. The steward was a household manager entrusted by the master of the house with the responsibility of taking care of things for him. The grace of God that Paul had described at such length had been given to him for this specific purpose.

As Paul had indicated in 1:9, the inclusion of the Gentiles was a mystery—something no one could have foreseen. But now the secret was open because God had revealed it to Paul in his conversion and call to missions. In verse 6 Paul summed up the mystery for his readers: "This mystery is that through the gospel the Gentiles are heirs together with Israel, members together of one body, and sharers together in the promise in Christ Jesus."

The content of the mystery is Christ—Christ for us in giving his life on our behalf and now Christ in us—accomplishing His purpose by working in each member of His Body.

This mystery is received spiritually (Eph. 3:4–5) and demonstrated in the proclamation of the gospel. Part of the mystery involves the disclosure that Gentiles share in the blessings of the gospel (2:11–13).

Paul Made a Minister (vv. 7–13)

Paul's Ministry

In verse 6 Paul mentioned the focus of his ministry. This was not something he chose for himself; he *was made* a servant of the gospel by God. He considered himself the "least of all God's people" (v. 8). This was not likely a false modesty on his part.

Before his conversion, Paul was one of the leading persecutors of the church. For him to become a minister of the gospel was a complete reversal of his life's course and not his own accomplishment. This happened through the working of God's power. Paul referred to his appointment as a "gift of God's grace." The purpose of his appointment was "to preach to the Gentiles the unsearchable riches of Christ and to make plain to everyone the administration of this mystery" (vv. 8–9). Paul traced this mystery all the way back to creation.

God's Plan

God chose to unfold His wise and wonderful plan in the arena of the church. Here we see God's work of redeeming and unifying taking place. One result of this revealing process taking place is the church, God's plan was made known to the "rulers and authorities in the heavenly realms" (v. 10). Angels, both good and bad, were learning about God's grace as it was being revealed in the church. God's plan to undo the work of evil power was successful.

The unsearchable riches of Christ are matters that far surpass our human ability to understand. In a doxology in his letter to the Romans, Paul described God's riches. Using this same word in Rom. 11:33, Paul exclaimed, "Oh, the depth of the riches of the wisdom and knowledge of God! How unsearchable his judgments, and his paths beyond tracing out." God's riches are so vast that no one can plumb their depths.

"Manifold wisdom"

Paul used an interesting word to describe God's wisdom. The word translated "manifold" is a compound word made up of the prefix *much* or *many* and the word *many-sided*. It conveys an idea that is difficult to express in English. It describes something as being "(very) many-sided," "many-faceted," or "many-colored." Paul wanted his readers to understand that this wisdom was richly diversified: "The idea in this word is that the grace of God will match any situation which life may bring us. There is nothing of light or of dark, of sunshine or of shadow, for which it is not triumphantly adequate"(William Barclay, *The Letters to the Galatians and Ephesians* [Philadelphia: Westminster, 1976], 127).

The Believer's Access to God

God's plan, however, was more than a successful operation. It became a personal experience. In Christ we have a free approach to God. "Rather than being overwhelmed by the greatness and power of God's magnificent plan, the believer in Christ finds himself in a close personal relationship with God. Christ gives him the boldness and confidence to come to God in faith" (David C. George, *2 Corinthians, Galatians, Ephesians,* Layman's Bible Book Commentary [Nashville: Broadman & Holman, vol. 21, 1979], 113).

■ *The purpose of Paul's appointment to the*
■ *ministry is "to preach to the Gentiles the*
■ *unsearchable riches of Christ, and to make*
■ *plain to everyone the administration of this*
■ *mystery" (vv. 8–9). God chose to unfold His*
■ *wise and wonderful plan and reveal the*
■ *divine mystery in the arena of the church. It*
■ *is here that we see God's work of redeeming*
■ *and unifying taking place.*

PRAYER AND PRAISE (3:14–21)

Paul's Prayer of Intercession for His Readers (vv. 14–19)

Paul now returned to the prayer he began in verse 1 and prayed that his readers would experience strength through the Holy Spirit and grasp the depth of God's love for them. Obviously, his vision of God's grand grace and the blessings of Christ moved Paul to an attitude of humility and prayer.

Paul again referred to God's "glorious riches." From such vast resources God can supply all the

Paul's Five Petitions for His Readers in 3:16–19

PETITION	PURPOSE
1. Inner strength	That God may work in them and through them
2. Faith	That Christ may dwell in their hearts
3. Love	That they may exercise a new orientation toward others
4. Spiritual understanding	That they may grasp the dimensions of God's love
5. The fullness of God	That they may personally and fully experience God's power

needs of His people. These are resources which His people may draw upon in prayer. Having defined this resource, Paul went on to ask for several blessings from these riches to be given to his readers. Paul made five requests for his readers:

1. Inner strength (v. 16)
The "inner being" is the center of a person's life. Herein lies a person's real strength. The believer's strength comes from God, who is present and active in a believer's life. His power works in and through the believer.

2. "That Christ may dwell in your hearts through faith" (v. 17)
The strength God gives is Himself, which Paul explains with his request "that Christ may dwell in your hearts through faith."

3. A new orientation toward others (v. 17)

With a new inner strength and the presence of Christ dwelling within, the believer has a new orientation toward others. Love is the foundation of the believer's life, and so Paul requested in this prayer that his readers be "rooted and established in love."

4. Spiritual understanding (v. 18)

Paul wanted his readers to comprehend the dimensions of Christ's love. His request was that they "may have the power to grasp how wide and long and high and deep is the love of Christ." The word for "power" is a compound word that conveys the sense of being "thoroughly strong" or able to grasp Christ's love. They are to exert this strength and power until they comprehend the dimensions of the love of Christ.

5. To be filled with the fullness of God (v. 19)

This is God's ultimate purpose for the lives of His people. God's Spirit dwells in believers, and the Christian life is a process of growth to this end.

Surpass

The word "surpass" is a compound word made of the preposition "beyond" and the verb "to throw." It means to throw over and beyond, and it is translated "surpass" or "excel."

In verse 19, Paul further explained that this love of Christ "surpasses knowledge."

Christ's love excels beyond and surpasses what one might gain through knowledge. Paul wanted his readers to have more than an intellectual knowledge of God; he wanted them to experience the fullness of God.

Paul's Doxology of Praise (vv. 20–21)

Paul's letter to the Ephesians reached a climax at this point. He delivered a stirring benediction, assuring his readers that God's power at work within them was able to carry out His work more abundantly than they could imagine. The wonderful news to Paul's readers is that this power was *working in them!* This power is active in all believers, and it is a means of glorifying God.

- *Referring to God's "glorious riches, Paul*
- *informed his readers that God can supply all*
- *the needs of His people. Paul went on to ask*
- *for several blessings from these riches to be*
- *given to his readers. A stirring benediction*
- *emphasizing God's infinite power working in*
- *His people closes this section.*

QUESTIONS TO GUIDE YOUR STUDY

1. What did Paul mean by "divine mystery"? What is the content of this mystery?

2. What was Paul's attitude toward ministry? What might we learn from his attitude and teaching about service to God?

3. What did Paul mean when he said that God's riches are "unsearchable"? That His wisdom is "manifold"? In what ways do these truths affect the Christian? How should the believer respond to these truths?

4. In desiring that his readers understand the dimensions of Christ's love for them, Paul prayed for his readers and made several requests on their behalf. What do we learn from Paul's prayer about the dimensions of Christ's love?

"Immeasurably more"

Paul used an extraordinary word to describe God's power to work on behalf of Christians. It is a compound word constructed of three words to show the highest form of comparison imaginable. Paul connected the words *above, out of,* and *exceedingly* to form this word. It means "exceedingly abundantly, superabundantly, quite beyond all measure, infinitely more." The idea the apostle conveyed here is that God's power is a concept that goes beyond the expression of language. It exceeds what we can "ask or imagine" (v. 20).

Chapter 4 began the second half of Paul's letter. Chapters 1–3 discussed the spiritual privileges of the church, spelling out the great Christian truths. In the last three chapters, 4–6, Paul drew out the practical implications and responsibilities that follow from the truths of the gospel.

THE UNITY OF THE CHURCH (4:1–6)

A Worthy Life (vv. 1–3)

Paul strengthened his appeal to his readers by referring to himself as a "prisoner of the Lord" (v. 1). His response to God's grace had resulted in his being in prison chains. What Paul urged his readers to do summarized all that he would write in chapters 4–6. He compared the Christian life to a walk, then asked them to "walk worthy of the calling to which you have been called" (NRSV).

Paul informed his readers that they had a calling. He placed the Christian life in a category beyond that of a gift or privilege; a calling comes from someone who has the right to claim loyalty. Here it implies that Christian living is goal-oriented and dynamic.

This calling, however, is more than simply a vocation or mission. To Paul, it was to a way of life—the Christian walk. He went on to define this walk in terms of attitudes and actions, listing four virtues. These same four virtues also appear in Paul's letter to the Colossians (3:12). These virtues are not to be static qualities; they are to be dynamic actions. Christians are to exercise:

Urge

The word Paul used here is translated "urge" by the *New International Version*. It is translated in other versions as "beg" or "exhort." In the original Greek text, this word is a compound made up of the preposition "alongside" and the verb "to call." It means "to appeal to, exhort, encourage." "The word signifies a will of the writer that is at the same time warm, personal, and urgent" (Fritz Rienecker, *Linguistic Key to the Greek New Testament* [Grand Rapids: Zondervan, 1980], 530).

- humility of mind;
- a gentleness with patience; and
- a bearing with one another in love.

Paul emphasized these virtues of the Christian walk:

Humility

Because the ancients did not have a word for humility that was not degrading, Christians gave new meaning to this word. People who are humble consider themselves "small," but at the same time they recognize God's power and ability working in them.

The New Testament writers regularly took the best words available to express new realties and put meaning into those words by the way they lived. In this way, they had a transforming influence on their society and its language.

Gentleness

This was another word for "meekness." However, it is not a synonym for weakness. It was used to speak of a wild animal that had been tamed, suggesting controlled strength or power under control.

Patience

This involves endurance and the attitude Christians are to show toward others as well as suffering. "Bearing with one another" is the practical expression of patience. *Patience* stays with someone until the problem or provocation is past.

Love

The background quality to the three preceeding virtues is *love* (see 3:17). In bearing with others, love accepts and overlooks another's weakness and loves others in spite of their faults.

All these virtues relate to and support the unity of the church. The unity Paul spoke of here is not organizational unity. Rather, it is a dynamic, living union of believers energized and united by the Holy Spirit who already indwells them. Those who are part of the body of Christ are to "make every effort to keep the unity of the Spirit through the bond of peace" (v. 3).

- *Paul compared the Christian life to a walk,*
- *asking his readers to walk worthy of the call-*
- *ing to which they have been called. He went on*
- *to define this walk in terms of attitudes and*
- *actions, listing four dynamic virtues that*
- *ought to characterize every believer in Christ.*

All in One—Unity (vv. 4–6)

Paul now turned his attention to the great spiritual realities that unite all Christians.

One Body (v. 4)

The church is the body of Christ. With Christ as its head, the body cannot be divided. Christ's body includes the redeemed of all time as well as local assemblies of believers. Believers everywhere should strive to achieve unity with each other in regard to primary truths and values.

One Spirit (v. 4)

There is one Holy Spirit who unites a group of believers. In each believer, the same power and person is at work. Paul had already made it clear (1:13) that anyone who has received Christ has received the Holy Spirit.

One Hope (v. 4)

Paul's mention of the Spirit led him to an affirmation of hope. Christians everywhere share in the call of God to His great purpose. All look ahead to the same future; all pursue the same goal.

One Lord (v. 5)

At the heart of Christian experience and faith is Christ, who is the "one Lord." Just as the spokes of a wheel are held together and arranged around a common hub, so all Christians come together around the one Lord.

One Faith (v. 5)

The original meaning of "faith" was the common commitment believers have to one Lord. The idea of faith as personal trust and commitment gradually extended to faith as a body of truths to which Christians adhere.

One Baptism (v. 5)

Baptism signals the beginning of the Christian life. Although there is much disagreement about the form and meaning of baptism, all believers share in this act.

One God (v. 6)

This is the central item in the list—the foundation piece. The ultimate basis for all unity is the oneness of God.

The "Oneness" of Believers in Christ

Unifying Factor	Key Idea
One body	All believers are part of a body of which Christ is the head
One Spirit	The same power and person is at work in all believers
One hope	All believers have the same future and pursue the same goal
One Lord	At the heart of every believer's Christian experience and faith is Christ

The "Oneness" of Believers in Christ

UNIFYING FACTOR	KEY IDEA
One faith	The common commitment believers have to one Lord
One baptism	Signals the beginning of the Christian life and an act which all believers share
One God	The foundation piece; the ultimate basis for all unity

■ *In this section Paul focused on the great spir-*
■ *itual realities that unite all Christians and*
■ *provided a sort of checklist of unifying fac-*
■ *tors that bind all believers together. The cen-*
■ *tral item in the list is the oneness of God, the*
■ *ultimate basis for all unity.*

BUILDING UP THE BODY OF CHRIST (4:7–16)

Each Member of the Body Given a Gift (vv. 7–10)

Having spent the first part of this chapter on the theme of *unity* in the body, Paul next turned to the idea of *diversity* within the body. Each believer has been "given grace according to the measure of Christ's gift" (v. 7, NRSV). This idea of measure suggests that the gift is individually tailored to each Christian.

To further develop this idea, Paul cited Ps. 68:18. The phrase "this is why it says" is a literary device, a formula that "introduces a citation from the Old Testament and is characterized by the absence of a legalistic and polemic undertone. It is an urgent invitation to listen attentively" (Fritz Rienecker, *Linguistic Key to the Greek New Testament* [Grand Rapids: Zondervan, 1980], 531).

Christ's Ascending and Descending

Paul further explained that his reference to Christ's ascending implies that He had first descended. This descent seems to correspond to His emptying Himself and coming in the flesh to dwell among people and to die (Phil. 2:5:11; John 1:1–18). Two other interpretations of the verse are sometimes proposed. Some interpreters think the descent was what was described in 1 Pet. 3:19 and that it refers to a visit to the realm of the dead between Christ's death and resurrection. Others suggest that this descent was the coming of the Holy Spirit at Pentecost. Paul emphasized the fact that the one who ascended was the same as the one who descended. This seems to have been aimed at the early false teachers who said the glorified Christ could not have experienced real human life and death.

The impact of Eph. 4:8–10 is that Christ—by His incarnation, death, resurrection, and ascension—had become available to fill all things ("fill the whole universe" (v. 9). He is able to give His people all that is needed to fulfill their calling (David C. George, *2 Corinthians, Galatians, Ephesians*, [Layman's Bible Book Commentary, vol. 21], 119).

Psalm 68:18 describes God returning in triumph after the defeat of the enemies of His people. As was the custom of returning conquerors, He led a parade of captives as He returned. The original Hebrew text reads, "Receiving gifts among men." Paul rendered that phrase here in Ephesians as "he . . . gave gifts to men" (v. 8). There is some evidence that Jewish writers quoted Ps. 68:18 with this same variation. The point of Paul's quoting this passage from the Old Testament is to show that Christ has ascended as conqueror of sin and death, and from His wealth He has given gifts to His people.

Spiritual Gifts Given to the Church (vv. 11–12)

In verse 11 Paul named the gifts Christ has given to His church. Of course, in general terms, Christ's gift to the church is the Holy Spirit (Acts 1:8). But the Spirit Himself is said to give a variety of gifts. Paul categorized these gifts in terms of functions that they perform in the church and those who perform those functions.

Apostles

In its most basic meaning, an *apostle* is a delegate, envoy, or messenger—a "sent one." The apostles were the original witnesses of Christ's life, death, and resurrection. Their function was to give a true representation of the gospel and to launch the missionary movement.

Prophets

These were persons who were recognized as speaking with authority. Their words were especially important before the New Testament writers became available to the churches to interpret the will of God. Prophets were able to speak the word of God in special situations to foretell (Acts 11:28; 21:9, 11), to convict (1 Cor. 14:24–25), and to encourage (Acts 15:32).

Evangelists

These were persons who proclaimed the gospel to those outside the church or to new regions. Philip is called an evangelist in Acts 21:8, and Paul encouraged Timothy to do the work of an evangelist in 2 Tim. 4:5. Today we would call such a person a missionary.

Pastors and Teachers

The word "pastor" means "shepherd." Paul's "image of a shepherd with his flock pictures the relation of a spiritual leader to those committed to his charge" (Fritz Rienecker, *Linguistic Key to* the *Greek New Testament* [Grand Rapids: Zondervan, 1980], 531). A *teacher* is one who instructs others in the way of truth. Paul linked *pastor* and *teacher* and, therefore, may have viewed them as a common group; that is, as *teaching shepherds*. Certainly, the church needs both functions within the body.

All of these persons and functions aim at the purpose Paul described in verse 12: "To prepare God's people for works of service, so that the body of Christ may be built up until we all reach unity in the faith and in the knowledge of the Son of God." The *New Revised Standard Version* translates the word *prepare* as "equip."

The verb form of this word is used in Matt. 4:21 to describe the mending or preparing of nets and in Gal. 6:1 to refer to restoring Christians to spiritual health. It designates a "fitting or fully preparing" (*Vine's Complete Expository Dictionary of Old and New Testament Words* [Nashville: Thomas Nelson, 1996], 467).

Paul's Lists of Spiritual Gifts

Spiritual Gifts	Rom. 12:6–8	1 Cor. 12:8–10	1 Cor. 12:28	1 Cor. 12:29–30	Eph. 4:11
Apostle			v. 28	v. 29	v. 11
Prophet	v. 6	v. 10	v. 28	v. 29	v. 11
Teacher	v. 7		v. 28	v. 29	v. 11
Pastor					v. 11
Miracles		v. 10	v. 28	v. 29	
Discernment of spirits		v. 10			

Paul's Lists of Spiritual Gifts

SPIRITUAL GIFTS	ROM. 12:6–8	1 COR. 12:8–10	1 COR. 12:28	1 COR. 12:29–30	EPH. 4:11
Word of wisdom, Knowledge		v. 8			
Evangelists					v. 11
Encouragers	v. 8				
Faith		v. 9			
Healings		v. 9	v. 28	v. 30	
Tongues		v. 10	v. 28	v. 30	
Interpretation		v. 10		v. 30	
Ministry/ Serving	v. 7				
Administration			v. 28		
Leaders	v. 8				
Helpers			v. 28		
Mercy	v. 8				
Giving	v. 8				

■ *All members of the church have received spir-*
■ *itual gifts for use in the fellowship. Leaders of*
■ *the church are to prepare all people for the*
■ *works of service so that the entire body might*
■ *experience growth and unity.*

The Church's Goal: Spiritual Growth (vv. 13–16)

Unity in the Faith

Paul emphasized this part is verses 3–6. Unity grows out of the common faith which believers share.

Unity in Knowledge of the Son

This kind of knowledge speaks about that which is directed toward a particular object. In this case, it involves knowing the Son of God. By knowing Christ intimately, believers experience Him as the one who knows God's character and brings God's presence as no one else does. In addition, this knowledge serves to bind Christians together in unity.

Maturity

The word "mature" carries the idea of being complete or reaching the goal. For the church to reach its goal of Christlikeness, it must have members who are attaining God's will for their lives. This kind of maturity is necessary if there is to be unity in the church. Paul contrasted this maturity with instability in verse 14: by comparing those who are "tossed back and forth by the waves, and blown here and there by every wind of teaching and by the cunning and craftiness of men in their deceitful scheming."

The Whole Measure of the Fullness of Christ

A complete person is one who measures up to the pattern of personhood displayed by Jesus Christ. This involves far more than our human standards or definitions of maturity. The fullness of Christ means all that Christ wants in the lives of His people.

Believers are not to be like those Paul warned about in verse 14. Those who use "cunning and

Cunning

The word "cunning" means "wicked dice playing" and refers to someone involved with intentional fraud. In contrast, those who follow Christ are to speak "the truth in love" (v. 15). By holding both truth and love in balance, Christians grow to be like Christ in their practical living.

craftiness" are deceivers and manipulators of the immature.

Paul closed this section by shifting his focus from the church and its members to the subject of Christ as the head and the parts of the body working together. All the members with their various gifts depend on Christ, the head. The body's growth and effectiveness depend on all members of the body working together. Again, Paul emphasized love as the means and manner for building up the church.

- *The church's gifts are to be used so that "the*
- *body of Christ may be built up" (v. 12). Paul*
- *taught a process that moves toward the goal*
- *of Christlikeness, and he described four parts*
- *of the process: unity in the faith, unity in*
- *knowledge of the Son, maturity, and the*
- *whole measure of the fullness of Christ. The*
- *body's growth and effectiveness depend on all*
- *members of the body working together, hold-*
- *ing truth and love in balance.*

PUTTING ON THE NEW NATURE (4:17–24)

Paul's opening phrase, "So I tell you this," was an urgent signal to his readers that what he was about to say was important. He used this attention getter to give a warning: "You must no longer live as the Gentiles do" (v. 17).

The Gentiles' minds were completely out of touch with the reality of God, so they were going nowhere. Not only did they lack understanding; they were hard-hearted, blind, shameless, and greedy. Paul pointed to the Gentiles and said, "You're not to be like this. This is the exact opposite of what Christ is."

Rather, believers need to do the following:

1. *Put off the old self (v. 22).* The way the believer puts off the old self is likened to the way one might put off clothes. The tense of the verb signifies a once-for-all, concluding action. The putting off is done once, permanently.

2. *Be made new in the attitude of the mind (v. 23).* This change is not only outward, but it also involves the inner person. The present tense of the infinitive "to renew" emphasizes that spiritual renewal taking place is a continuing process.

3. *Put on the new self (v. 24).* The word for "put on" is also used in the sense of putting on a garment. Indeed, the NRSV translates this passage, "Clothe yourselves with the new self." This new self is "created according to the likeness of God" (v. 24, NRSV). This verse might possibly mean that a new self is created in God's image.

■ *Becoming a Christian involves far more than*
■ *learning truths with the mind. It requires a*
■ *complete break with the past life of sin. The*
■ *person who believes in Christ takes off the*
■ *old, corrupted self and then puts on the new*
■ *self, which is created to be like God.*

The Commands of 4:25–5:2

Most of the commands in this passage are in the present tense. The present tense with the command indicates that the actions of the verbs used are to be habitual. This applies to both negative and positive commands. This formula in use with positive commands means that the reader is to continually act in a certain way. In the case of the command "Be imitators of God," the believer is to continually imitate God. It is to be a habit. This formula used with negative commands, such as "Do not grieve the Holy Spirit of God," is considered a *prohibition*. This particular prohibition means that the person grieving the Spirit, is to *stop* doing so, and is to *continue* not grieving the Spirit.

EXAMPLES OF THE NEW WAY OF LIFE (4:25–5:2)

In this very practical and challenging section, Paul focused on holy living. Believers are to walk in purity as well as unity. The apostle first showed negatively how believers should not walk and issued several commands to his readers.

Walking in the New Way

Aspect	Command, Prohibition, or Entreaty	Reason
"Put off falsehood and speak truthfully" (v. 25)	Commands	For we are members of one body
"In your anger do not sin" (vv. 26–27)	Prohibition	So the devil will not gain a foothold
"Steal no longer" (v. 28)	Entreaty	To work honestly and help those in need
"Do not let any unwholesome talk come out of your mouths" (v. 29)	Prohibition	So that we may exhibit God's grace to others and build them up
"Do not grieve the Holy Spirit" (v. 30)	Prohibition	We are God's vessel and the temple of the Holy Spirit
"Get rid of all bitterness [and] rage" (v. 31)	Entreaty	So we may maintain and cultivate good relationships
"Be kind and compassionate" (v. 32)	Command	So we may be considerate and meet the needs of others
"Be imitators of God" (5:1–2)	Command	So we may exhibit the nature of God in word and deed to our world

Paul suggested several positive aspects of Christian conduct.

Speaking the Truth (v. 25)

Falsehood is not a characteristic of the believer's new nature. Not only are we to put away lies; but also our lives are to be characterized by speaking the truth. Because Christians depend on one another, they must be able to trust other's words and deeds.

Dealing with Anger (vv. 26–27)

Paul quoted Ps. 4:4, "In your anger do not sin." It is a Hebrew way of saying, "When you are angry, do not sin." This command is not a license to anger. Paul recognized that anger is a part of life and must be handled realistically and constructively. Paul urged believers to settle negative feelings before sundown. A failure to do so keeps one's anger alive and provides the devil with a "foothold"—room to work his evil in a person's life.

"Paul's antidote for a habit of taking is to develop a habit of giving" (David C. George, *2 Corinthians, Galatians, Ephesians,* [Layman's Bible Book Commentary, Vol. 21], 125).

Honest Work (v. 28)

Hands that were previously involved in stealing must now engage in honest work. Paul advocated a change in behavior. Those who were inclined to dishonest gain by stealing should stop that kind of behavior immediately, replacing it with hard work and giving to others in need.

Gracious Speech (v. 29)

Becoming a Christian changes the way a person speaks. Speech controlled by the new nature will exhibit three characteristics:

1. It edifies or builds up.
2. It is appropriate.
3. It has a redemptive effect on those who hear it.

"But this is what you must do: Tell the truth to each other. Render verdicts in your courts that are just and that lead to peace. Do not make evil plots to harm each other. And stop this habit of swearing to things that are false. I hate all these things, says the Lord" (Zechariah 8:16–17, NLT).

Harmony with the Spirit (v. 30)

The new nature at work within the believer is the work of the Spirit. God is saddened and disappointed when His people fail to live up to their new nature. The Spirit is grieved. The Spirit is the seal and guarantee of the believer's future complete redemption. (For a review of the Spirit's ministry of sealing, see 1:13.)

Christlike Relationships (v. 31)

Immediately following his warning against grieving the Spirit, Paul listed six forms of sin that must be put away. These sins are normally expressed within the context of speech, and all six involve relationships with others. The following chart lists these sins and their specific meanings.

Six Sins of Speech

SIN	EXPANDED MEANING
Bitterness	A spirit of resentment that refuses to be reconciled
Rage	A subtle, deep-flowing, persistent antagonism against someone
Anger	A temporary outburst of temper
Brawling	Loud expressions of grievance, shouting
Slander	Speaking evil of others and God
All malice	A general term that includes any evil word or act against another; the root of the above vices

Being Imitators of God (5:1–2)

Paul challenged his readers to the highest standard possible: "Be imitators of God." He taught that what Christians became when they believed on Christ, they must diligently continue in their daily behavior. He challenged his readers with two commands: "Be imitators of God," and, "Live a life of love."

"Be imitators of God" (v. 1)

If we are to be like God, we must imitate Him. This command is in the present tense, indicating that this should be a continuous, ongoing action by the Christian.

"Live a life of love" (v. 2).

Paul highlighted two areas in which believers are to imitate: by exercising love and forgiveness toward others.

■ *In this very practical and challenging sec-*
■ *tion, Paul focused on holy living. Believers*
■ *are to walk in purity as well as unity. The*
■ *apostle first showed negatively how believers*
■ *should not walk and then issued several com-*
■ *mands to his readers.*

QUESTIONS TO GUIDE YOUR STUDY

1. Paul listed several character qualities in verse 2. How do these equip the believer to fulfill Paul's command in verse 3?

2. What was Paul's point in verses 4–6? What is the foundation or key unifying factor of this "oneness"?

3. Paul mentioned several spiritual gifts. How does each contribute to the growth of the body of Christ? What does the

"Dear friend, don't let this bad example influence you. Follow only what is good. Remember that those who do good prove that they are God's children, and those who do evil prove that they do not know God" (3 John 11, NLT).

Imitator

The term *imitator* was understood by Paul's readers. "Imitation was the main part of the training of an orator. The teachers of rhetoric declared that the learning of oratory depended on three things—theory, imitation and practice. The main part of their training was the study and the imitation of the masters who had gone before. It is as if Paul said: 'If you were to train to be an orator, you would be told to imitate the masters of speech. Since you are training in life, you must imitate the Lord of all good life'" (William Barclay, *The Letters to the Galatians and Ephesians* [Philadelphia: Westminster, 1976], 160–61).

word "equip" mean? What is the goal of spiritual growth?

4. Contrast the believer's old and new natures. How does a person "put on" the new nature?

5. What changes take place when a person puts on the new nature?

6. What did Paul mean by urging Christians to imitate God?

This chapter continues Paul's instruction on the Christian walk. His main topics are warnings against immorality, instruction on walking in wisdom, and submission within the marital relationship. Because 5:1–2 logically is part of the closing section of chapter 4, it is treated there.

FURTHER WARNINGS AGAINST SIN (5:3–14)

Immoral Behavior and Talk (vv. 3–7)

After his summary statement in 5:1–2, Paul appeared to double back and attack the sins of the pagan world. This served to emphasize the urgency of the problem Paul saw. Here he listed several sins, the first of which are concerned with sexual immorality:

Fornication. This refers to illicit sexual activity or sexual activity outside of marriage. From the Greek word for" fornication" we get the English word *pornography.*

Impurity. This is a broad term for immorality or uncleanness.

Greediness. This word was often used to describe uncontrolled sexual desire.

Paul next shifted to sins of conversation:

Obscenity. This refers to shameful, filthy, or obscene speech.

Foolish Talk. Known as the "talk of fools," it is the conversation of the drunkard.

Coarse Joking. This is the language that makes light of human weakness or human goodness and ultimately tears down the quality of life.

Paul declared that his readers should not make these topics a matter of conversation and should not associate with people who practice and talk about these things: "Do not be partners with them" (v. 7). To underscore the seriousness of this kind of immoral behavior, Paul stated that those who practice these evils will not share in the inheritance of the kingdom of God.

Light and Darkness (vv. 8–14)

Light, because it is the nature of Christ, is powerful. Paul provided some specific details about the light that Jesus Christ brings to humankind.

Light produces good fruit (v. 9).

Paul listed goodness, righteousness, and truth as the products of light. Those who walk in the light exhibit a spirit of generosity.

Light exposes motives (v. 10).

Light enables the Christian to discriminate between what is pleasing and what is not pleasing to God. It is in this light that all motives, attitudes, and actions must be tested. Believers are to "find out what pleases the Lord."

Light exposes evil (v. 12).

Light exposes the unfruitful works of darkness. Evil activity, when dragged into the light of Christ, is seen for what it is and dies a natural death.

Light cleanses (v. 13–14).

Although this (v. 13) is a difficult verse to interpret, it seems that Paul declared that light has a cleansing effect. What is exposed by the light becomes influenced by the light. In addition to the light's function of condemning evil, light has a healing effect. Certainly, light is a witness to people in darkness. The effect of

Believers Are Light (v. 8). Believers walk in the light, and evildoers live in darkness. Believers themselves once "were darkness, but now in the Lord are light" (v. 8, NRSV). Because of their standing in Christ, Paul urged his readers to "live as children of light." Another way of saying this is, "Try to learn what is pleasing to the Lord." The guiding rule in this walk is whether an attitude or action is pleasing to God.

light on a sinful heart can result in the healing of the soul.

Contrast Between Darkness and Light

Darkness	Light
Produces lies (v. 6)	Embraces truth (v. 9)
Produces sin (v. 6)	Produces righteousness (v. 9)
Unfruitful (v. 11)	Produces fruit (v. 9) (goodness, truth, righteousness)
Shameful (v. 12)	Pleasing to God (v. 10)

To conclude this section. Paul introduced an indirect quotation from Isaiah 60:1: "Wake up, O sleeper, rise from the dead, and Christ will shine on you." This quotation includes the name of Christ, leading most scholars to believe that it is from an early Christian hymn.

This passage from Isaiah describes the beginning of the Christian life as waking from sleep, as rising from the dead, and as receiving light. Certainly, those who have experienced Christ cannot take part in the ways of sleep, death, and darkness.

- Paul attacked the sins of the pagan world
- and listed sins of sexual immorality and sins
- of conversation that Christians are to avoid.
- Not only are believers to avoid evil deeds;
- they are also to avoid associating with those
- who practice such deeds.

WALKING IN WISDOM (5:15–20)

The way believers conduct their Christian walk is critical. They are to exercise wisdom. In light of their redemption from darkness into light, they must take decisive steps. Paul addressed his readers with several exhortations. He did this to appeal to the will, the volitional side of a person. Paul intended that these exhortations guide believers into patterns of wise living. It was his desire that they develop the following qualities in their Christian lives.

The Christian Walk of Wisdom

AREA	PAUL'S EXHORTATION
	Walk carefully
Opportunities for doing good	Seize opportunities
God's guidance	Understand God's will
Control and stability	Be filled with the Spirit
Encouraging one another	Speak praises to one another

Walk Carefully (v. 15)

The idea Paul conveyed here is that of looking around carefully to avoid stumbling and falling.

Christians are to be aware and alert, taking advantage of the light they have in a dark world.

Seize Opportunities (vv. 15–16)

"Redeeming the time" is how other versions have translated this phrase. Paul is teaching here that wise living involves making the most of our time. The kind of time Paul spoke of here is not the passing of hours, days, and years, but strategic time in the form of windows of opportunity. Timely action is especially important because "the days are evil."

Understand God's Will (v. 17)

Understanding God's will is directly related to understanding God's Word. God's will as revealed in His Word is always the criterion and the motivation for Christian living.

Be Filled with the Spirit (v. 18)

The key idea of the word *filled* is control. The indwelling Spirit of God ought to be the dominant and controlling factor in a believer's life. Those not controlled by the Spirit are vulnerable to evil influences and will ultimately give way to control by their own lusts and desires.

Sing Praises to God (v. 19)

The early church was a singing church. Paul described the gathering of believers as they were filled with the Spirit. "Psalms" refers to the songs of Israel in the Old Testament, and "hymns" may have been new songs of the Christian faith. While these spiritual songs were shared among believers, their purpose was to praise God. This praise was to be accompanied with thanksgiving, a quality possible only to those whom God had redeemed through Jesus Christ His Son. From Scripture we find that the early church was indeed a thankful church.

Redeeming the time

The New Revised Standard Version translates Paul's phrase in verse 15 as "redeeming the time." The word for "redeeming" ("seize," NIV) is a compound word made up of the preposition "out" prefixed to the verb "to buy." This compound means "to buy out." The "time" Paul refers to is "a season" of time. Opportunities that cannot be recalled are missed. Believers are to grab each opportunity for doing good, turning it into the best advantage for the cause of Christ.

- *The way believers conduct their Christian*
- *walk is critical. This involves taking decisive*
- *steps. Paul addressed his readers with sev-*
- *eral exhortations to guide them into patterns*
- *of wise living.*

WIVES AND HUSBANDS (5:21–33)

PAUL'S WRITINGS ON THE MARRIAGE RELATIONSHIP

Eph. 5:22–6:4
Col. 3:18–21
1 Cor. 7:1–17
1 Tim. 2:8–15

Reverence for Christ

In speaking of reverence, Paul used the word for "fear." This is not the kind of fear that arouses alarm or terror. Rather, it is the biblical meaning of the word to indicate profound respect. A reverential fear of Christ will inspire a constant care and consideration in one's dealings with others. This is important because the submission of both husband and wife to Christ's authority will ensure proper attitudes within the relationship.

Mutual Submission (v. 21)

Paul exhorted believers to be submissive to one another: "Submit to one another out of reverence for Christ" (v. 21). Although in the following verse Paul applied this exhortation to husbands and wives, he did not limit his emphasis to the husband-wife relationship. His emphasis on unity and harmony applies to the entire body of Christ.

Counsel to Wives (vv. 22–24)

Wives are to submit to their husbands in everything: "Submit to your husbands" (v. 22). The term "submit" means "to be subject to."

This word is common to specific New Testament instruction regarding the relationship between husband and wife (see Col. 3:18; 1 Pet. 3:1, 5). It is "used in a military sense of soldiers submitting to their superior or slaves to their masters. The word has primarily the idea of giving up one's own rights and will, i.e., 'to subordinate one's self'" (Fritz Rienecker, *Linguistic Key to the Greek New Testament* [Grand Rapids: Zondervan, 1980], 538).

The term for "submit" is also used in a variety of other contexts, including the subjection of all things to Christ, the subjection of persons to civil authorities, and the subjection of one Christian to another. In his *The Epistle to the Romans*, C. E. B. Cranfield, speaking of this subjection, stated, "It is the responsible acceptance of a relationship in which God has placed one and the resulting honest attempt to fulfill the duties which it imposes on one" (p. 662).

Submission has nothing to do with worth before God or before each other. Submission does not imply inferiority. Rather, it is an expression of a God-ordained role. Verse 23 is critical. The wife is to be subject to her husband because the husband is head of his wife in the same way that Christ is head of the church. The husband is the God-appointed leader of the home, and he is held accountable for that role.

Counsel to Husbands (vv. 25–33)

Paul's command to husbands was: "Love your wives" (v. 25); and he immediately told husbands what it meant to do so. Paul pointed to Christ and said in effect, "You see how much Christ loved the church? You see how he demonstrated that love to the church? In that way—to that degree—you husbands are to love your wives."

- Paul exhorted believers to be submissive to
- each other, and then he made a special appli-
- cation to the husband-wife relationship.
- Wise believers, filled with the Spirit, who
- mutually submit to each other contribute to
- the unity and harmony of the entire body of
- Christ.

QUESTIONS TO GUIDE YOUR STUDY

What difference would it make in your home, if the wife were subject to the husband in all things, and the husband puts the good of his wife ahead of his needs and wants in every decision and action?

1. Paul listed several sins of immorality and conversation. What was his point?
2. Paul exhorted believes to walk in the light. Contrast this spiritual light with spiritual darkness. What does the light that Christ brings accomplish in the life of the believer? How does it affect the unbeliever?
3. What are some of the steps of walking in wisdom?
4. Paul urged his readers to "seize opportunities" and "redeem the time." What are some ways Christians can do this?
5. Regarding Paul's teaching on submission, what was his counsel to wives? To husbands? What does *submit* mean for the wife in the context of the marital relationship?

Continuing the theme from the previous chapter, Paul began this final chapter by providing counsel for children and parents, slaves (or workers) and masters. He then shifted to the subject of spiritual warfare and God's provisions for the believer's battle against evil.

Counsel to Children (vv. 1–3)

Paul's counsel for children came in the form of two commands: obey and honor. Both should be exercised continuously.

"Obey your parents" (v. 1)

Children are to obey the instruction of their parents. Paul added a reason: "For this is right." This phrase could have more than one meaning. It could mean that a child's obedience is recognized as right by all people. Or it could mean that a child cannot always understand the reasons for a parent's instructions and must obey because it is the right thing to do.

"Honor your father and mother" (v. 2)

To honor something is to value it or revere it. Here Paul cited the Fifth Commandment: "Honor your father and your mother" (Exod. 20:12). "Honor" is a broader word than "obey." In the case of younger children, it calls for obedience. In the case of older children, it calls for respect and care for the parents.

Counsel to Parents (v. 4)

Paul included a word to parents. He probably used the word "fathers" in a general sense that would include both parents. He delivered his counsel in the form of one negative command and one positive command.

Children and Parents (6:1–4)

Paul first focused on the relationship between children and their parents. He emphasized that there is to be harmony in the home, and he provided counsel for both children and parents.

Obey

The Greek word translated "obey" is a compound word made up of the prepositional prefix "under" and the verb "to listen, attend." This word is also translated "to submit." It describes the proper response in certain kinds of relationships, such as children to parents and servants to masters.

Biblical Instruction from Paul for Children

Passage	Form of Instruction	Counsel
Ephesians 6:1–3	Command	"Children, obey your parents in the Lord."
Colossians 3:20	Command	"Children, obey your parents in everything."
Exodus 20:12 (The Fifth Commandment)	Command (Quote from the Old Testament	"Honor your father and your mother."

Training and instruction

The word *training* speaks of discipline used to correct transgressions of laws. The word *instruction* literally means "a putting in mind." It is often translated "admonition" and refers to verbal instruction. *Instruction* is "the training by word," whether of encouragement, or, if necessary, by reproof. (Taken from *Vine's Complete Expository Dictionary of Old and New Testament Words* [Nashville: Thomas Nelson, 1996], 13).

"Do not exasperate your children." (v. 4b)
Parents are not to "exasperate" or provoke their children to anger. Their exercise of authority is not to be harsh. Rather, parental authority is to be exercised with due regard for the child, recognizing the child's rights and feelings.

"Bring them up in the training and instruction of the Lord."
To "bring up" a child is to nourish and care for that child. Parents are to raise their children in the training and instruction of the Lord.

■ *Paul addressed the relationship between*
■ *children and parents. Children are to obey*
■ *their parents. Parents are to exercise their*
■ *authority with due regard for their children*
■ *and bring them up in the training and*
■ *instruction of the Lord.*

SLAVES AND MASTERS (6:5–9)

Counsel to Slaves (vv. 6–8)

The Roman world lived with slavery. From the earliest times, the government accepted and promoted the practice. In the Roman world, treatment of slaves varied considerably. By the first century, however, the institution of slavery was changing. Public sentiment was against harsh treatment of slaves, and many leading orators spoke against the institution. This caused many masters to free their slaves.

Christianity arose in a real-life, tension-filled setting. The slaves' insurrections had already failed, causing significant injury, sorrow, and loss of life. Working within these tensions, however, the seeds of abolition were sown.

In the Roman Empire of Paul's day, nearly all work was done by slaves. A large portion of the population consisted of those in forced servitude either as captives of the Romans or as debtors unable to pay their obligations. It is likely that many early Christians were slaves. Therefore, Paul included Christian instruction for those in slave–master relationships. His approach to the slavery problem of his day was to urge both slaves and masters to acknowledge Christ as their Lord.

Paul's words "whether he is slave or free" remind us today that Paul's instruction is just as applicable to the modern-day employee as to the first-century slave. He urged workers to:

Obey with respect and sincerity (v. 5).

Servants are to obey their masters in the same way they obey Christ. Paul mentioned qualities of this obedience:

- *Respect and fear.* This phrase elsewhere is translated "with fear and trembling" (NRSV).
- *Sincerity.* This word conveys the ideas of simplicity, uprightness, and "singleness of heart" (NRSV).

Serve wholeheartedly (v. 7).

Paul instructed that service to masters should be done wholeheartedly, as if the servants were serving the Lord directly. Christians are serving Christ, even in their daily duties. This word suggests a good will that does not wait to be compelled to action.

When Paul wrote to Philemon encouraging him to take back his runaway slave, Onesimus, the apostle said, "For perhaps he was for this reason parted from you for a while, that you should have him back forever, no longer as a slave, but more than a slave, a beloved brother, especially to me, but how much more to you, both in the flesh and in the Lord" (Philemon 15–16, NASB).

Counsel to Masters (v. 9)

There was much cruelty and abuse of slaves in the Roman Empire, but Christian masters were to be different. They were to do good to their slaves. Their relationship with their slaves was to be governed by the awareness of their accountability to God for what they did. In situations where both slave and master were Christians, they were in a master–slave relationship at one level. But at a more important level, they were equals as brothers in Christ.

■ *In this passage, Paul addressed the relation-*
■ *ship between servants and masters. Servants*
■ *are to obey their masters and serve them*
■ *wholeheartedly. Masters are to treat their*
■ *servants with goodness. Both are to conduct*
■ *themselves as if they were serving Christ*
■ *Himself.*

THE WHOLE ARMOR OF GOD (6:10–20)

Paul concluded his letter to the Ephesians by preparing his readers for the spiritual conflict of life. He made them aware of the enemy, Satan, and exhorted them to put on the "armor" that God supplies so they may be equipped for the battle.

The Believer's Fight Against Evil (vv. 10–13)

Paul's use of the word "finally" indicated to his readers that he was beginning to draw his letter to a conclusion. It drew together several themes from throughout the letter but particularly pointed to 5:3–18, where Paul described evil deeds and evil days as enemies of God's people. Paul began his instruction with three commands: "Be strong in the Lord," "put on the whole armor of God," and "take your stand against the devil's schemes."

"Be strong in the Lord" (v. 10).
Paul exhorted believers to be strengthened or empowered for the battle. Human effort is not enough; the strength and power for the fight must come from God, His "mighty power." The Christian draws strength from:

- Realizing that believers are seated with Christ "in the heavenly realms" (1:19–23), a much higher position than Satan and his principalities; and
- The fact that the power of God is available to every believer through the power of the indwelling Spirit (3:14–21).

"Put on the full armor of God" (v. 11).
To put on the armor of God is to clothe oneself with the necessary equipment for battle. It is important to include all the parts of the armor to protect oneself completely from the attacks of the enemy.

Stand

The word *stand* "could be used in a military sense indicating either 'to take over,' 'to hold a watch post,' or it could also mean 'to stand and hold out in a critical position in a battlefield' (Barth)" (Fritz Rienecker, *Linguistic Key to the Greek New Testament* [Grand Rapids: Zondervan, 1980], 541).

> *"Take your stand against the devil's schemes" (v. 11).*

Just as an enemy will come up with a variety of schemes to try to gain victory in combat, so it is with Satan against God's people.

Satan, The Enemy

HIS WEAPON	PASSAGE	OUR DEFENSE
Crafty schemes	Eph. 6:11	Putting on the full armor of God and standing against the enemy
Strategy and devices	2 Cor. 2:5–11	Confessing our sins, forgiving others, and claiming God's forgiveness for ourselves
Snares	1 Tim. 3:7	Maintaining a good testimony among the unsaved
Ignorance and lies	2 Cor. 4:1; Luke 22:53	Not succumbing to Satan's power and authority

The Believer's Equipment for Battle (vv. 14–17a)

In this graphic passage, Paul pictured the Christian soldier being outfitted for a battle. To wage this battle with human effort is foolish. The believer must put on God's full armor in order to be strong "in his mighty power." Human effort is inadequate in spiritual warfare, but God's power is invincible.

Armor is essentially a shield worn directly on the body. Since the body is most vulnerable in the head and chest regions, it was especially there where armor was worn. Saul and Goliath wore helmets (1 Sam. 17:5, 38), as did the entire army of Judah, at least in the time of Uzziah (2 Chron. 26:14). The helmet was usually made of leather or metal. It was designed in various shapes depending on the army and even on the unit within the army so the commander could distinguish one unit from another while viewing from a higher vantage point. The different helmets helped the soldier tell whether he was near an enemy or comrade in the confusion of tight hand-to-hand combat.

With the rise in popularity of the arrow with its speed and quickness, the mail came to be more and more necessary to cover the torso. Fish-scalelike construction of small metal plates sewn to cloth or leather was the breastplate for the ancient soldier. These scales could number as high as seven hundred to one thousand per "coat." Each coat obviously could be quite heavy and expensive to produce in volume. The distant enemy units of archers who might find themselves firing on each other would wear mail, along with archers riding in chariots. While in a chariot, Ahab was hit and killed by an arrow exactly where the mail was least protective—at the seam where the sleeve and breast of the coat met (1 Kings 22:34). Leg armor, like the bronze leglets of Goliath (1 Sam. 17:6), was not regularly used in Old Testament times.

Arms and armor surfaced on only a few occasions in the New Testament. In New Testament times Roman imperial soldiers were equipped with metal helmets, protective leather and metal vests, leg armor, shields, swords and spears.

The armor of God is both the armor He supplies and the armor He Himself uses in the battle. Paul listed the items in the order in which they would be put on. He identified each one by the spiritual quality each represents. Because Paul emphasized the "full armor of God," the details of the individual pieces should not be pressed too far.

Truth

Christians who go to war against the lies of Satan, the father of lies, must not be tripped up by their own untruth.

The first step in preparing for battle was to gird the loins. Because men in ancient times wore long robes, their movement in battle or work could be hindered. To eliminate this hindrance, they would pull up the robe and tie it about the waist and hips with a girdle or belt. Paul says this belt is *truth*, which means sincerity of character.

Righteousness

In battle, the breastplate was vital, for it protected the heart and lungs. This is what *righteousness* does for the believer.

Peace

Shoes are important to the foot soldier. For the Christian, it is the gospel of peace that makes his feet spring lightly across the field or makes it possible for him to stand firmly in position when such a stance is required. Just as shoes provide foundation to our standing or moving, so the gospel is the foundation on which we stand.

Faith

A shield was indispensable for battle. The kind of shield Paul spoke of was large enough to cover the body, about two-and-one-half feet by four feet in size. These shields were made of leather and were often soaked in water to ensure protection from flaming arrows. The Christian's shield is faith, which is a complete confidence in God's power. It is important to note that to "take up" the shield (v. 16) does not mean to grab with one's own strength; rather, it is a *receiving* of what is given by God.

Salvation

The helmet protects the most vital and vulnerable part of the body—the head.

This willingness to let God work in the believer's life can effectively protect one from all the enemy can deliver.

"The Roman soldier wore a bronze helmet equipped with cheek pieces. The helmet was a heavy decorative and expensive item that had an inside lining of felt or sponge which made the weight bearable. Nothing short of an axe or hammer could pierce a heavy helmet" (Fritz Rienecker, *Linguistic Key to the Greek New Testament* [Grand Rapids: Zondervan, 1980], 542).

Therefore, the helmet of salvation is the Christian's most basic protection. Armed with God's grace and the guarantee of eternal life, the Christian soldier can remain fearless. Nothing the enemy will do can break the bond that holds the believer to God. Although believers may experience setbacks during the battle, they will be able to hold their heads up when the battle is over

The Believer's Preparation Through Prayer (vv. 17b–20)

Two offensive weapons are included with the armor of God: (1) the "sword of the Spirit," which is the Word of God, and (2) prayer.

A Christian's basic defense against evil is obedience to God's Word and will and an uprightness in his or her conduct. Improper attitudes and actions become "kinks" in the armor—weak areas through which the enemy may thrust his weapons.

The Sword of the Spirit" (v. 17)

The kind of sword Paul described is the short, straight sword the Roman soldier used. It was used as a close-range weapon. The sword given by the Spirit to be wielded as an offensive weapon is the Word of God. God's sword has life and power, and we learn from Heb. 4:12

that it never grows dull. Indeed, it is a very effective weapon, "piercing until it divides soul from spirit, joints from marrow; it is able to judge the thoughts and intentions of the heart" (NRSV). Christians learn to conquer the enemy on the spiritual battlefield when they understand Scripture, apply its life-changing truths to themselves, and obey it commands and precepts..

The Armor of God

ARMOR PIECE	SYMBOL	MEANING
Belt	Truth	Sincerity of character
Breastplate	Righteousness	Uprightness in conduct
Shoes	Peace	Gospel of peace
Shield	Faith	Complete confidence in God's power
Helmet	Salvation	God's grace and the guarantee of eternal life

Prayer (v. 18)

Prayer is what energizes the Christian. Paul set forth several guidelines for this prayer. The Christian is to pray:

- in the Spirit;
- on all occasions; and
- with all kinds of prayers and requests.

The attitude of the prayer warrior should be one of alertness and persistence. It is to be constant and intense. Like a guard keeping watch over

On many occasions, Jesus urged His disciples to watch and pray. In Luke 18, Jesus told a parable to His disciples "to show that *at all times* they ought to pray and not to lose heart" (Luke 18:1, NASB).

the camp, the Christian is to be vigilant without a letdown.

Paul concluded this section by describing himself as "an ambassador in chains" (v. 20). He was in prison, wearing iron prison chains. In Paul's time, Rome housed many ambassadors in fine embassies. Paul, an ambassador of Christ, found himself imprisoned. Because ambassadors normally would not be arrested, Paul indicated the wrong he was suffering.

- *Paul concluded his letter to the Ephesians by*
- *preparing his readers for the spiritual con-*
- *flict of life. He used the Roman soldier's*
- *weapons and armor as images to express the*
- *virtues necessary to defend the believer*
- *against Satan. To ensure victory, the Chris-*
- *tian warrior is to put on the full armor of*
- *God and to use the sword of the Spirit and*
- *prayer on the spiritual battlefield.*

PAUL'S FINAL WORDS TO HIS READERS (6:21–24)

Acknowledgments (vv. 21–22)

At the end of his letter, Paul acknowledged the personal ties between himself and some of his readers. He would send a special messenger, Tychicus, to hand deliver the letter. Verses 21–22 are nearly identical to Col. 4:7–9, indicating that Tychicus carried both letters.

Benediction (vv. 23–24)

The book closed with a rich benediction. Familiar themes of peace, brotherhood, love, faith, and grace are the blessings Paul pronounced on God's people. He spoke eloquently of Christ's

Be Alert

The word Paul used in verse 18 for "be alert" (better translated "keep alert," NRSV) means "to stay awake, to lie sleepless, to be watchful, vigilant." The grammatical elements of this verb speak of continuous, unbroken action. This command is coupled with the word "persevere" (NRSV), intensifying the action. From our study of papyrus documents of New Testament times, we know that the verb form of *persevere* was used to describe "waiting until one's trial came before the court or diligently remaining at one's work" (Fritz Rienecker, *Linguistic Key to the Greek New Testament* [Grand Rapids: Zondervan, 1980], 543).

love for His church. At the end he graced them with the title, "All who love your Lord with an undying love." By "undying" Paul meant a love that is incorruptible, not only in its endurance but also in its character.

- *Paul's final words to his readers were an*
- *acknowledgment of his personal ties with his*
- *readers and a benediction.*

QUESTIONS TO GUIDE YOUR STUDY

1. Regarding harmony in the family, what is Paul's counsel to children? To parents? Explain his commands to both.

2. How should Paul's instruction in verse 4 affect a parent's attitude and behavior toward his or her child or children? How does a parent bring up a child "in the training and instruction of the Lord"?

3. Paul included counsel for the slave-master relationship. What was his counsel to both, and what of his counsel is applicable to our modern work environment?

4. Describe the believer's fight against evil. What commands did Paul give his readers to prepare them for the battle?

5. Describe God's armor for fighting the battle. What does each part of the armor represent? What offensive weapons does God provide the Christian warrior?

The following list is a collection of the works used for this volume. All are from Broadman & Holman's list of published reference resources. They meet the reader's need for more specific information or an expanded treatment of Ephesians. All of these works will greatly aid in the reader's study, teaching, and presentation of Paul's Epistle to the Ephesians. The accompanying annotations can be helpful in guiding the reader to the proper resources.

Adams, J. McKee (Rev. by Joseph A. Callaway), *Biblical Backgrounds*. This work provides valuable information on the physical and geographical settings of the New Testament. Its many color maps and other features add depth and understanding.

Blair, Joe, *Introducing the New Testament*, pp. 151–56. Designed as a core text for New Testament survey courses, this volume helps the reader understand the content and principles of the New Testament. Its features include special maps and photos, outlines, and discussion questions.

Cate, Robert L. *A History of the New Testament and Its Times*. An excellent and thorough survey of the birth and growth of the Christian faith in the first-century world.

George, David C. *2 Corinthians, Galatians, Ephesians* (Layman's Bible Book Commentary, vol. 21), pp. 91–140. A popular-level treatment of several of Paul's epistles, including Ephesians. This easy-to-use volume provides a relevant and practical perspective for the reader.

Holman Bible Dictionary. An exhaustive, alphabetically arranged resource of Bible-related subjects. An excellent tool of definitions and other information on the people, places, things, and events of the Bible.

Holman Bible Handbook, pp. 711–18. A comprehensive treatment that offers outlines; commentary on key themes and sections; and full-color photos, illustrations, charts, and maps. Provides an accent on the broader theological teachings of the Bible.

Lea, Thomas D. *The New Testament: Its Background and Message,* pp. 437–447. An excellent resource for background material—political, cultural, historical, and religious. Provides background information in broad strokes on specific books, including Ephesians.

McQuay, Earl P. *Keys to Interpreting the Bible.* This work provides a fine introduction to the study of the Bible that is invaluable for home Bible studies, lay members of a local church, or students.

McQuay, Earl P. *Learning to Study the Bible.* This study guide presents a helpful procedure that employs the principles basic to effective and thorough Bible study. Using Philippians as a model, the various methods of Bible study are applied. Excellent for home Bible studies, lay members of a local church, and students.

Robertson, A. T. *A Grammar of the Greek New Testament in the Light of Historical Research.* An exhaustive, scholarly work on the underlying language of the New Testament. Provides advanced insights into the grammatical, syntactical, and lexical aspects of the New Testament.

Robertson, A. T. *Word Pictures in the New Testament,* "The Epistles of Paul," vol. 4, pp. 516–552. This six-volume series provides insights into the language of the New Testament Greek. Provides word studies as well as grammatical and background insights into the epistles of Paul, including Ephesians.

SHEPHERD'S NOTES

SHEPHERD'S NOTES

SHEPHERD'S NOTES